CHRISTIAN FAITH SERIES

CONSULTING EDITOR: *Reinhold Niebuhr*

Man's Knowledge of God

Man's Knowledge of God

BY WILLIAM J. WOLF

HOWARD CHANDLER ROBBINS PROFESSOR

EPISCOPAL THEOLOGICAL SCHOOL

Doubleday & Company, Inc.
Garden City, New York, 1955

Library of Congress Catalog Card Number 55–5261

To my wife ELEANOR
and to our children
EDWIN, JOHN, and STEPHEN

Contents

Man's Knowledge of God

The Search for "God" Today

There have been a number of surveys conducted in recent years to determine what people mean by the word "God." It would be interesting to add a second question: "Where do you find God?" The results would have more than academic interest; they would lead directly into the major problems and moods of our generation.

"God" is again becoming popular. There is an increasing production of books about religion, and a surprising number of these are found on best-seller lists. This development presents a sharp contrast to the situation in the twenties and thirties when interest in religion sank to a low ebb. This popular return to "God" might be described simply as the swing of the pendulum whereby a human interest that has been crowded out in one generation returns in another, destined to be relegated to the background in the succeeding one. There are, however, signs at hand that something much more serious than a cyclic interest pattern is before us. It can variously be assessed as the awakening of man to the reality of his situation after a "haunted sleep" or as a "failure of nerve" before the gigantic political and social problems of our day. It may be

neither of these simple alternatives but a confused mixture of the
two.

"God" seemed an irrelevant appendage in an age confident that
all problems could be solved by human ingenuity. Man was very
much in the center of things because he had put himself there with
great apparent success. Western Europe and the United States
were, except for minor skirmishes, enjoying a period of world peace
from the last decades of the nineteenth into the first decades of the
twentieth century. Even World War I could be described as the
"war to end all wars" and as the "war to make the world safe for
democracy." These comfortable illusions largely informed the educational philosophy of the West in the twenties and early thirties,
leaving the growing generation unprepared for the events it would
have to face. The growth of democratic institutions became a key
principle for interpreting the history of Europe in textbooks which
were actively in use when the rise of Fascism, Nazism, and Soviet
Communism belied this oversimplification. Apparently man would
not always choose the rational democratic answer. Shortly before
the turn of the century Spencer saluted the inexorable march toward progress and human perfectibility by citing the abandonment
of torture as evidence of modern man's superiority to his forbear-
ers. What would he say about the murder of millions of Jews at the
hands of a racialist raised to the helm of a great modern state? How
would he square his faith in man with the newer tortures that de-
prive man of the opportunity to be a martyr for his principles? Certainly scientific advance and technological progress were solid
facts, but the instruments forged in this advance make possible
tyranny of proportions hardly imaginable before. In the buoyant
optimism of those halcyon days "God" seemed an excess piece of
theological baggage destined to be cast aside by the streamlined
man of tomorrow. The message of the Church about the sinfulness
of men, the danger of pride, and the need for redemption seemed
outmoded.

The mood of our day in contrast is a chastened one. There is,

Change of attitude argued for God

however, still a strong undercurrent of optimism ready to respond
to any new device only to experience frustration and despair when
it crumbles. It may be that the return to "God" expresses in some
degree this hope for a new handle to solve man's problems. Educational theory, scientific methodology, and enthusiasm for democratic institutions are not now "the current method." Perhaps the
new method is religion and "God." Perhaps these new resources
will make our difficult problems more capable of solution, or perhaps they will compensate us by "peace of mind" from feeling
that we must face them at all. Moving into a suburb where the
issues of modern living are standardized may point to the desir-
ability of having "a God" as one should have a shiny new car or a
swimming pool. One of the basic dictionary definitions for God is
"an idol." Perhaps a generation that has discovered the clay feet
of its idols of materialism, progress, humanism, and technocracy
now projects its uncertainties into the sky in the unconscious hope
that this new "God" by definition will not have clay feet. This
"God," however, might still be a new idol.

It is easy to caricature the swelling Hooper rating for "God" and
to interpret it as "compensation" for a bad case of contemporary
jitters. On the other hand, the renewed interest in things religious
may express a genuine conversion of values. The hollowness of the
self-sufficient man may have become so obvious that it yields to a
new openness to God. It may indicate that a new sense of proportion in assessing the nature of man is at hand. The French saying,
"from divinity, through humanity, to animality," seems clearer to
us than before. There are undoubtedly many honest seekers after
"God" who feel that only from the perspective of religious faith can
the catastrophic events of our day be understood or our responsibilities in them find meaning and purpose. These people do not
wish to dictate what that meaning shall be. They are open and
hopeful that "God" will disclose the essential meaning of things.

In such a mixed situation as has been described the common element is the word "God." There is a widespread assumption that

this word must have some recognizably common features. People talk about "God" and assume that others will know what they mean. That assumption has a limited validity. The word "God" has a social, communal inheritance behind it, conditioned by the cultural domination of Christianity for nearly two thousand years in what is so often naïvely called "the Christian West." The word "God" achieved a very specific content during that time. Many modern people who have lost the distinctively Christian content of the word still use it assuming it has some agreed residual content. It meant for the Christian "The Lord God" who is one of a kind, utterly self-existent and majestically supreme, the Living God who discloses his will in the Biblical narratives. It has apparently come to mean for many modern people one of a class of objects called "God." Whereas Christianity knew only "God" and "idols," modern man, feeling that such an exclusivist terminology was intolerant, has employed the word in ways that suggest a plural or at least other members of the same class. To each his own "God." We are confronted with a semantic problem that wins a prize for subjective individualism. It is surprising how often one hears such statements as "every one should be free to worship *his own* God" or "if there is *a* God . . ." The use of the indefinite article and the personal possessive adjectives especially in the singular number testify to this basic shift in the meaning of the word "God." Partly it may result from denominational pluralism in the Christian churches. Partly it expresses new meanings given to the word "God" in the last two centuries that have dissolved or eroded its traditional meaning. "God" has been described as "a quality of the universe that makes for growth" (Wieman). "God" is the mathematical principle discernible in the construction of the universe (Jeans). "God" is the "conservation of values" (Ames). "God," as described by John Dewey in *A Common Faith,* is the relation between the ideal and the real, capable of further actualization in experience. "God" is "a universal obsessional neurosis" of mankind stemming from the "oedipus complex" (Freud). With S. Alexander in *Space,*

Time, and Deity "God" is "an emergent who aspires to existence." "God" for most people, said Dean Inge, is a "cosmic blur." In other words, "God" in our day *is what we make it mean.*

A recent study of Thanksgiving proclamations disclosed an interesting fact. The further back one went the more the sentiment expressed was humble gratitude that God in his infinite mercy had vouchsafed these blessings to our undeserving people. The more recent ones, however, struck the note of congratulating the deity for his wisdom in allying himself with such enterprising and successful people as we Americans.

The confusion that cloaks the use of the word "God" by modern man needs to be dispelled before we can really ask the question "What do we know about God?" But the problem is more complicated than this. Where we look for "God" will partly determine what we mean by "God." And the direction in which we look for "God" may be determined by an absent-minded habit inherited from an age of faith that makes little sense without the presuppositions of that faith.

The complexity of these issues may be clarified by some artless testimony from a member of Alcoholics Anonymous. The man described his growing addiction to alcohol that threatened both his business and his marriage. He wanted to stop drinking but could not. He sought out an acquaintance who had been cured and asked his help. The friend urged him to get down on his knees and pray when the craving pressed upon him. "I can't do that because I don't believe in God. It would be ridiculous for me." "Do you believe in anything stronger than yourself?" asked his friend. With a nod at the double-decker bus grinding past in the street he said, "I believe that bus is stronger, more powerful than I am." His friend, notwithstanding the fantastic quality in the suggestion, urged him to pray to that bus when he felt overwhelmed by the craving for alcohol. The man testified that in his desperation he did just that and that he felt an accession of strength not his own. "I continued," he said, "and when I found it intolerable to pray to a bus I changed to calling it 'Harry'. Soon I realized that the unseen helper could only fitly be called 'God'."

This simple odyssey from the personification of material forces through some invisible person to God is an eloquent testimony to the power of prayer. It is doubtful if man can long pray to impersonal forces or subpersonal entities. Prayer is a test for the living awareness of God as personal. The more significant element here for our consideration is that this experience took place within a society that had been molded by Christianity. Would this experience have been duplicated in a Hindu society? It certainly would not in these terms at least, for to the Hindu mind the personal is by no means the highest value in life. The personal is regarded as belonging to the realm of the illusory and the contingent. In other words, while there is nothing explicitly Christian in the experience as described it presupposed the belief that God must be personal just because that is the conditioning belief that molded the total context within which the experience took place.

This point is especially important because most people today in the West who speak about "God" generally presuppose considerable elements of personality even when curiously enough they say that they have met this "God" in areas of human experience where "the personal" is not likely to be disclosed. The reason may be that their unrecognized dependence upon a religious tradition is actually stronger with them than their verbally described experience of "God" in the areas where they are accustomed, they say, to find him. Or if the unconscious inheritance is not stronger, it has provided the glasses through which they see things which they mistakenly report seeing with the naked eye.

What is meant here can be illustrated by a survey made recently of some sixty people who had met for group Bible study, most of them for the first time in their lives. The leaders of the groups were especially skillful in eliciting the beliefs and disbeliefs of the participants in utter frankness. A majority said that they did not agree with the claim of their Church that God was primarily re-

vealed in Jesus Christ. They felt they had an experience of him
directly in the beauty of nature. Many of them stated that working
around their grounds away from other people, from the confusion
of the family, and from the killing pace of business and social
activity they found the quiet and beauty of nature sacramental of
the presence of "God."

If questioned, "Where do you find God?" probably a majority of
people would begin with the world of nature. Aesthetic considerations might be paramount and they would describe the beauty of
a sunset over a snow field, or the limitless horizons of the oceans,
or spring flowers beside a swollen brook, or the rich tapestry of
autumn colors. The peace of nature, especially against the hurly-
burly of modern living, would give them a feeling of the presence
of "God." Others would respond less to the peace of nature than to
its gigantic power. The terror of a volcanic eruption, the incredible
power of erosion as shown in the Grand Canyon, an icefall in some
rugged intermountain basin would evoke feelings of awe and reverence for the power of "God." In both these characteristic experiences "nature" could have been substituted, as it often is by many,
for the word "God." The long tradition of pantheism, the view
that nature itself is divine, in critical and popular philosophy has
argued that "God" and "nature" are interchangeable words. Yet
many of those whose experiences have been described would object strongly to the use of the word "pantheism." Some are aware
that pantheism as a philosophy or a religious system destroys in-
dividuality and swallows up the personal. Most of these people
would argue that their experiences of "God" in nature have elements of the personal about them. The language they use betrays
this fact. They will use the third personal pronoun to designate
"God" and will presuppose specific content when they ask questions about God. They assume often, for example, that love must
be one of God's attributes.

Strictly from the data of nature before them there is no ground
either for the assumption that "God" is personal or that "He" pos-

sesses attributes of love. Where in all the majestic spectacle of nature is there any evidence that God loves? Is it not rather that nature exhibits a supreme indifference to man? Is not the "peace" of nature the result of a selection of some specialized data at the expense of the evidence pointing to the struggle and wastage in the evolutionary process? "Nature red in tooth and claw" is conveniently omitted from consideration. The insecurity of man in the face of hostile forces of nature, his tragic vulnerability to disease and accident—are not these also part of the picture? It might be argued that behind nature, if we cannot postulate a God of love, we can at least have the assurance that "God" is a "he" and not an "it." The old deistic argument of finding a watch on the ground and then arguing to the existence of the watchmaker has been restated in terms of data from recent scientific investigations. The argument never achieves completely demonstrable certainty; it may achieve a high order of probability. There is, however, other data from scientific research which in the hands of those bent on disproving "God" or his personal qualities gains impressive degrees of probability. In short, our situation with respect to the evidence for the existence of a personal God from the facts of nature, whether in the form of the traditional cosmological argument that stresses the necessity for a first cause or in the form of the teleological argument that centers on the evidence of purpose in the world, remains problematic. Judged strictly as arguments or proofs, they neither prove nor disprove the existence of "God." They do show us how the human mind is driven to find unifying principles for interpreting existence. Even if they did establish the existence of a superhuman intelligence, they could not demonstrate its goodness.

Comparatively few modern people have subjected their experience of finding "God" in nature to the critical tests of philosophical inquiry. It is the more interesting then to analyze why people have such confidence in so ambiguous a procedure. The reason must surely be that they are paying their expenses not from current salary but, without recognizing it, from their inherited capital.

They are not looking at nature with pristine eyes but with eyes of faith. That faith has come to them not from nature but from a historical community. They have imbibed from the culture in which they have been raised certain basic Christian presuppositions of faith which they have accepted uncritically. These presuppositions are so common that it takes a confrontation with people raised in other religious cultures (which unfortunately seldom occurs) to make them realize that these are not expressions of "common sense" or "universal presuppositions" but the special Christian conditioning of the word "God." God is discovered in nature by the Christian because he believes that God is the Creator and Sustainer of the world. The belief in creation was historically a corollary of the conviction that God disclosed himself primarily in history. When Jesus speaks of the lilies of the field and the fowls of the air or when the Psalmist testifies that the heavens declare the glory of God and the firmament his handiwork they speak from out of a special religious tradition in which God was disclosed to faith. Because it was believed in that tradition that God was the Creator, good and loving, they learned to find nature sacramental of his presence. When, therefore, a group of Church people claim that they find God in nature directly rather than where their official religious tradition claims to find him they must be challenged about the implication of the word "directly" and about their unconscious borrowing from the tradition they now verbally dispute. Their presupposed knowledge of God was mediated through history in its original development and it is so being mediated to them today although in weakened and attenuated forms. Richard Niebuhr summarizes this involved situation:

"We cannot point in space to spacial or in a general time to generally temporal things, saying that what we mean by word of God and by revelation can be known if men will but look together at stars and trees and flowers. It is with Kant in his time-space we must regard the starry heavens, and with Jeremiah see the blossoming almond, and with Jesus behold the lilies of the field before we can read words of God in nature's book. Nature regarded through our history is indeed a symbol of what we mean, a pointer to God, but nature uninterpreted through our history and faith, or torn out of this context and placed in another does not indicate what we mean. It means various things according to the point of view from which it is regarded and the context in which it stands— utter indifference to man and all his works in the context of despair, a blessing upon brutality from the point of view of confidence in military might, and a dominant interest in mathematics in the context of faith in mathematical thought as the only road to truth."[1] Others would not look to the data of nature to find "God" but to the existence in man of his moral consciousness. The inexorable majesty of the moral law is here the primary locus. God is the "good." One suspects that this approach had greater popularity about the turn of the century than it has in our day. The "God" of nature after all makes few moral demands on its followers. Immanuel Kant is the person chiefly responsible for opening up the "moral" path to "God" in conscious opposition to the path of "speculation" with its traditional rootage in the cosmological and teleological arguments. He argued that "God" is the necessary explanation of the universal sense of "ought." This quality that separates man from the most intelligent animals is regarded as the key to human self-understanding. The eclipse in popularity of this approach to "God" in our generation is caused by many factors. One of the most powerful is a growing sense of relativism about the dictates of conscience fostered by our increased knowledge of primitive societies and their contradictory taboos. The concept of a universal moral law has had its content whittled down almost to the vanishing point. The dubious interrelationship between the conscience and the unconscious drives in man, fully exploited by depth psychology, has made us increasingly skeptical of this avenue of approach. The force of the moral argument may be shown

[1] Richard Niebuhr, *The Meaning of Revelation,* Macmillan, 1941, pp. 48–49.

to rest not on the contradictory deliverances of conscience in various groups at various times but upon the sense of obligation to obey whatever is regarded as right and to avoid whatever is regarded as wrong, but the restatement does not appear to carry much conviction today. But even in the circles where "God" is found by this method, could not the phrase "moral law" be adequately used to account for the experience? Why import so questionable a theological term for an experience apparently so simple? The "God" disclosed here is the personification of morality. That there is in fact more meant here is another illustration of the bringing to experience of a presupposition from traditional Christian and Jewish belief in ethical monotheism. The chief reason for the loss of popularity of the moral approach is that it carried more conviction when the cultural background was still recognizably Christian. Today our pluralistic and confused background has considerably reduced what might once have appeared as a conclusion of "common sense."

God in history

Some have professed to find "God" behind the events of general history, representing him in Lowell's words as standing "within the shadow keeping watch above his own." The shadow has greatly deepened today. Evil has been on the throne too long. There is less conviction that the scaffold of truth "sways the future." A very impressive philosophy of history, including in its survey twenty-one civilizations, is being developed by Arnold Toynbee with progress in religion as its key principle. Civilizations collapse from pride and irresponsibility. Only the religious values of humility and brotherly concern can arrest the decline of our Western civilization. Toynbee's analysis and prescription is only conceivable on the basis of Jewish-Christian values in a culture made conscious of the problem of history by that very religious development. The Marxist interpretation of history with economic strife its key feature sees no hand of God in the clash between rival classes. Religion is regarded as a prescientific tool used by vested interests to keep the proletariat quiet. Many humanist evaluations of history

popular in the West with progress in rationality and goodness as
basic beliefs discover no grounds for the presence of "God" in the
process. As will be analyzed later, the Christian cultural conditioning is at its maximum in interpreting the meaning of history. The
knowledge of God that is presupposed, although in attenuated
form, by most modern people who claim to experience God directly in nature, conscience, or general history is the product of a
once vital faith in the living God who discloses himself in history.

To the fields already surveyed where modern man finds "God"
might be added an analysis of reason or of beauty or of universal
religious experience, but the total setting of the problem would
not be markedly different. The validity of finding "God" in these
areas is really dependent upon the prior validity of the Christian
knowledge of God. Experiences from these several fields converge
in fairly eloquent testimony to the fact of God's existence. They
do not provide constitutive knowledge about who he is. That modern man has uncritically assumed this constitutive knowledge, or,
more accurately, reduced expressions of this knowledge, suggests
the need for an inquiry into the original data behind the present
forms of the experience. What exactly does the Christian affirm
about God and about the areas of human experience that may become transparent for a knowledge of him? The question of modern
man about "God," from the very way in which he asks the question, is a question about the God of Christian experience. In the
light of the Christian knowledge of God the modern attempt to
find "God" in nature, history, and conscience then becomes more
understandable. To a consideration of the Christian community
and its knowledge of God we must now turn.

CHAPTER II

Where Christians Find God

The preceding chapter indicated that the silent presupposition behind much of the modern search for "God" is the inheritance of the Christian conviction that he reveals himself primarily in a historical community. Our generation is no stranger to the general problems of community in history. In a day when technological progress has made the simpler world of our grandparents a complex field of daily interaction we find ourselves struggling to bridge the currents of nationalism and ideological conflict. The United Nations and the European Coal and Steel Authority express the drive of historic forces toward the abridging of national sovereignties in the interest of a greater degree of world community. The obstacles that threaten these institutions and that are rationalized in the Charter of the United Nations vividly illustrate the more powerful forces that work against world community and which, if unchecked, will breed another global conflict. Our inability significantly to abridge national sovereignties mocks our conviction that abridgment is a prerequisite for survival. In such a situation men begin to ask questions about this curious creature whose mind rises above the conflicts of history and who

sees the need for world community, but then as a citizen of some
stubborn national unit is unable to achieve the solution so obvious
to his mind.

Many of those who are most concerned about this problem fail
to see another element in the picture. It is the simple fact that a
world Christian community already exists. The very fact of its
existence is an empirical reality tremendously significant for those
who struggle to modify the disruptive forces of our uneasy situation. But the immediate significance of this world Christian community is less startling than the questions which it raises about the
mysterious supranational loyalty that is at the heart of this
phenomenon. It sheds light also on the problematic creature who
lives in such a community of faith and at the same time remains
subject to the disruptive forces of his national community. These
last forces are so strong that they have fragmented the community
of faith into "churches" divided into national and racial groupings.
Considering how encumbered the world Christian community is
by these divisive forces of world history, it is not surprising that
many fail to assess correctly its significance. What are the facts
about this community, established in history, yet pointing to realities not immediately obvious on the historical plane? What, moreover, is their significance for man's *knowledge* of God?

A recent edition of an almanac lists 600,000,000 Christians.
Carrying the analysis further, it may roughly be calculated that
one out of every four people in our world acknowledges a nominal
Christian loyalty. The next most serious contenders for man's religious allegiance are Hinduism with 230,000,000 and Islam with
221,000,000. Confucianism is not listed because of the question
whether it is a religion or a national code of behavior. None of
these non-Christian religions has anything like the universal
spread of Christianity. To be sure, Christians are more concentrated in those areas of the globe in which our Western culture
developed, as in Europe, or to which it spread in the period of
colonial expansion, as in the two Americas and Australasia. Its

establishment in Africa and Asia coincides historically with the imperialist expansion of the European powers and the United States as agents of Western culture in an age now nearing an end. That Christian missions have been historically associated with the wave of Western aggression against the peoples of Asia and Africa has seemed a convenient "proof" to Communist propagandists that Christian missions are simply tools of the white man's aggression. To the average Westerner or Asiatic politician they may also be suspect as "cultural aggression." While it is true that missionary nationals of some Western powers enjoyed a special legal status in China because of unequal treaties, and that the British government of India was a help to Christian missions in establishing law and order and preventing a denial of religious liberty, the deeper analysis reveals a struggle by commercial interests protected by Western governments to eliminate or to circumscribe Christian missions in many areas of Asia and Africa. Furthermore, the emergence of movements for independence and the revolutionary ferment of ideas about self-government and democracy are due in no small measure to the indirect consequences of Christian teaching and example.

Today the Chinese Christian community is subjected to persecution by the Marxist regime. Increasingly serious obstacles may be placed by India and Pakistan on the freedom of their Christian subjects, but the significant fact here is that, despite the expulsion of Western governments and their imperialistic privileges, indigenous Christian communities within Asiatic countries continue to expand and to deepen their witness at a time when the nationalism of the "liberated" or newly independent countries increases world tension. What has happened is that a world Christian community finds indigenous expression in the nations that have rejected Western rule although they are busy imitating its vices of political nationalism and cultural pride. Here is a testimony to the vitality of the Christian faith and to the dynamism of its gospel that is not rivaled by any of the other world's religions. The purpose of this geographical analysis is not to advance the naïve idea that numbers determine truth nor to demonstrate from them thereby the superiority of Christianity. It is to illustrate the conviction that the empirical fact of such a world community, capable of sustaining itself under such varied historical configurations, calls for an analysis of the way such a community regards its task, of the sources of its strength even under persecution, and for any light it may throw upon contemporary problems.

The existence of a Christian community behind the rival "churches" is attested by the growth of the Ecumenical Movement in our generation, a movement dedicated to expressing the oneness of the Church throughout the *Ecumune*, or "the whole inhabited world." The "churches" have never quite been able to accept with complacency the divisions of Christendom. From the time of the final rupture between Latin Christianity and Greek Orthodoxy in 1054, through the turbulent multiplication of churches and sects in the Reformation period, to the co-operative missionary movements in the eighteenth and nineteenth centuries there have been numerous individuals and unofficial groups dedicated to the realization of Christ's prayer "that they may all be one . . . that the world may believe that Thou hast sent me."[1]

What is new in our day, beyond the acceleration of the movement for co-operation and unity, is that the churches have committed themselves officially to this task of reconciliation and that this co-operation has achieved fragmentary expression in the World Council of Churches and the International Missionary Council. There is a further difference in that most of the pioneering movements were pan-Protestant in orientation, whereas the modern Ecumenical Movement aims to include both the Catholic and Protestant traditions. The degree of success already attained in bridging the gap between two traditions often regarded as irreconcilable opposites as well as between churches of the same tradition yet separated by the bitterness of family quarrels raises

[1] John 17:21.

the question of how this movement could have come about. By what agreed formula do these rival churches co-operate?

The basis for their co-operation has involved agreement on a minimal but indispensable definition of what constitutes a Church. The Constitution of the World Council of Churches declares that it is a "fellowship of churches which accept our Lord Jesus Christ as God and Saviour." Even within the membership of the some 163 different churches in 48 countries there exists considerable difference as to whether other members can be accurately called "churches" and whether the confessional basis of "accepting our Lord Jesus Christ as God and Saviour" is adequate even as a minimal point of recognition and association. The really significant point here, however, is not the failure of the confessional formula to solve all tensions but the common agreement that this world Christian community recognizes that its reason for existence, its power to witness beyond the national divisions of our world, springs from its understanding of a historical event—the life of Jesus of Nazareth—regarded in faith as "Our Lord Christ" and as "God and Saviour." The formula sharpens up the significance of the fact that a supranational historical community explains its historical existence in terms of special attitudes toward a historical event at its foundation. The Christian knowledge of God is obviously centered about that event.

The observer who is trying to discover the clue to this world Christian community finds other interesting evidence in an expression of this community that goes beyond the principle of federative co-operation typified in the World Council of Churches. This further organizational expression is represented in one area of the world where an organic union has been established between churches of both Catholic and Protestant traditions. In 1947 occurred an event described by Dr. Henry Sloane Coffin as "the most significant ecclesiastical event since the Reformation." This was the foundation of the Church of South India as an organic union of churches of the Presbyterian, Congregational, and Methodist traditions with the Anglican Church that has retained the Catholic order of ministry in historical continuity. An examination of the constitution of this Church shows that it was constructed around the Lambeth Quadrilateral, a document emphasizing the Bible as the supreme rule of faith, the Gospel sacraments of Baptism and the Lord's Supper, the historic creeds as testimonies to that faith, and a historically continuous ministry represented by the episcopate. At the heart of this document is the decisive significance given to the Bible as expressing the faith of the community and to the Church as witnessing to that faith.

There are other signs that the Catholic-Protestant gulf is not quite so unbridgeable as was thought by the partisans of previous generations. There is the renewal of interest in Bible study within churches of the Catholic tradition. It has been expressed in recent papal encyclicals requiring regular Bible study of all priests and instruction of the laity in the Bible. It is also found in Greek Orthodoxy in such movements as "Aktines" and "Zoe" (or "Life") which are largely lay-inspired and lay-conducted courses in Bible study. The ancient Mar Thoma Church of India, descended from Syrian Christianity, has experienced a great renewal in group Bible study. Paired with this development has been the rediscovery by the Protestant churches of the importance of the doctrine of the Church in the New Testament as expressed in recent theological literature and in the choice of the Church as a topic for the Amsterdam and Evanston assemblies of the World Council of Churches. What is happening today is that Catholics are rediscovering the Bible and Protestants are rediscovering the Church. The Bible and the Church are understood more and more not as rivals but as expressions of an indissoluble organic relationship. It was a false perspective when the Bible was applied like a yardstick to the Church by Protestants unconscious of their own ecclesiastical presuppositions or special traditions of exegesis just as it was false for Catholics to regard the Bible as a past chapter or as simply one among many other elements in a holy tradition. This unnatural opposition between Church and Bible failed to see that the true center of attention in the Bible is the person of Christ, who is himself authoritative, rather than the documents about him. The true life of the Church, moreover, is not primarily a historic institutional succession but a life of fellowship in obedience to the Christ who is the head of his body, the Church. The Bible is not an external yardstick but stands related to the Church as an inner "spirit of the whole." The deeper point of association between Church and Bible is the person of Christ. Recent developments in both Catholicism and Protestantism raise in a new form the question of the meaning of the person of Christ as basic to any understanding of church life today.

Enough evidence has been presented to show that the churches today understand their inner principle to be the acknowledgment that God is uniquely present in Jesus of Nazareth. Here is where they find God. Is the universalism of this affirmation, with its impressive geographical distribution and growing ecumenical quality, matched by the same self-understanding vertically throughout the nearly two thousand years of the existence of the Christian community? Is there, in other words, a continuity of witness on this point, stretching across the centuries and rooted in the years immediately following the life of Jesus?

The answer to this question is an affirmative one. Historians who analyze the literary sources of our present gospels declare that the earliest sources are written from the point of view of their faith in Christ. All of the New Testament writers, however differently they express it, agree that "God was in Christ," that is to say, that God has disclosed himself uniquely in the person of Jesus. The Christological orientation of the gospel documents is paralleled by the basic message of St. Paul and by that of the primitive Christian community. "Jesus is Lord" is the earliest form of confession recorded in the Acts. The significance of the word "Lord" is not to be found in its use for the leader of a pagan cult but in its use in Jewish religious tradition which was here determinative for the early Christian community. In the Greek translation of the Old Testament the word "Lord" is used with reference to God himself. Hence the significance of this ascription is not that Jesus is the cult-leader but that he is somehow one with God himself. The name "Christian" given to the community at Antioch as a derisive label provides indirect testimony as to where even the opponents of Christianity saw the center of gravity to lie.

A classic illustration of this type of confession, this time in the language of Messiahship, is found in the incident at Caesarea Philippi, told by the three earliest evangelists. The "Messiah" means in Jewish tradition the expected, or "anointed," representative of God. The details vary, but the Matthew account, perhaps the latest, is especially interesting.[2] In answer to Jesus's question as to who the crowds think him to be, the disciples answer John the Baptist, Elijah, Jeremiah, or one of the prophets. Then the question is readdressed to the disciples themselves: "But who do *you* say that I am?" Then Peter says: "You are the Christ, the Son of the living God." In acknowledgment Jesus puns about the name Peter meaning "rock" and says, "On this rock I will build my church, and the powers of death shall not prevail against it." In terms of the evidence of the rest of the New Testament it is highly unlikely that Peter is here being granted a pre-eminent position like an Oriental caliph; what is most probably meant is that Peter's confession of faith in the person of Christ is to be the real foundation for the community of faith itself. This note is emphasized by Jesus's reply: "Blessed are you, Simon Bar-Jona! For flesh and blood has not revealed this to you, but my Father who is in heaven." It is an affirmation about a historical person, but it is not simply on the plane of "flesh and blood," but in the realm of a suprahistorical interpretation, i.e., "my Father . . . in heaven . . . has revealed this to you." The narrative then contains a warning against disclosing the Messianic secret. Jesus teaches that he must go to Jerusalem and there must suffer and be killed. Im-

[2] Matthew 16:13–20.

mediately the impetuous Peter protests against this statement and
the disciple who had just been praised as the mouthpiece of God's
revelation is now rebuked as "Satan" and as "a hindrance." Apparently there were dimensions to the Messianic task that Peter
had not understood.

The evidence shows a remarkable continuity of witness from
the period of the early Church to our own day when the churches
are again seeking a focus of unity in "Our Lord Jesus Christ as God
and Saviour." In this brief review there is already indicated the
primary area of examination for any inquiry into what man can
know of God. The Christian experience of God has a remarkable
unity of focus in history itself. Christians have not, in spite of the
well-known approaches of both Catholic and Protestant scholasticism, begun their quest for the knowledge of God by a series of
arguments drawn from nature or from conscience. These philosophical approaches were always in the nature of a rationalization
after the fact. That is to say, Christians have experienced God
within their historical community of faith and then attempted to
demonstrate that the God found within the community, the God
who disclosed himself in history, was also the Creator God who
had created the natural and the moral orders.

Any inquiry then into the Christian understanding of God is
compelled, if it would be faithful to the empirical evidence, to
examine those experiences of the historical community in which
it is believed that God reveals himself. This means a study of the
significant experiences behind the written records of the Old and
New Testaments. The next two chapters will therefore be concerned with the way in which these ancient documents should be
used. Further chapters will show that the Christian knowledge of
God focuses around Jesus Christ. This development will pose in a
radical way the question of history and the problem of faith. The
Cross will prove central to our knowledge of Christ. Subsequent
chapters will be about the community of faith that responds to
these events and about the contemporary task of the Church in

developing and deepening our knowledge of God. After such an inquiry it may then be necessary to show why Christians were driven into arguments for the existence of God from the evidence of nature, reason, and conscience. Another question that will obviously arise is the relation of the Christian knowledge of God to what may be known of him in the religions of mankind. The method of approach has been to begin on the shadowy peripheries of the current revival of interest in "God," to return to a study of the vital center in the Biblical tradition, and then to allow that center to illuminate our current problems.

The preceding review has established the rough dimensions of the area in which God's revelation is received by the community. It can be seen that "revelation" is the basic religious category. Just as the physicist employs the category of "mechanism" as an inclusive summation of physics, the biologist that of "organism" for his field of inquiry, and the psychologist "personality" in dealing with human selves, so the inquirer into what man can know of God who directs his inquiry toward the Christian tradition must reckon with "revelation" as the illuminative term.

New evidence in the field of physics, chiefly from a study of the structure of the atom as typified by Heisenberg's principle of indeterminacy, has directed criticism toward the older conception of mechanism. So it may also be discovered that time-honored ways of defining revelation within the Christian community or in systems of natural theology must be restated in the light of new evidence. If this is the situation the Christian believer is no more threatened than the physicist when he accepts change. The faith of both that each is in touch with reality may actually be deepened when the increasing relativity of the observer's position is understood.

The problem then is revelation. Enough material has been adduced, moreover, in the survey to suggest the broad outlines of a preliminary definition. Revelation is the knowledge of God springing from certain historical events and persons about which and about whom a special interpretation is made within the believing community. The problematic element here is the point at which the continuity of the plane of history is intersected by the plane of religious faith. It may prove helpful in describing this line of intersection to employ another formula from the field of science. That formula may be described as *continuity with discontinuity*, not a logical self-contradiction, but an expression for what the scientist Morgan tried to describe with his phrase "emergent evolution." The orders of existence, as they increase in complexity from the inorganic to the organic and from the organic to the self-conscious level, subsume mechanism under organism and organism under personality, without destroying the simpler form by the addition of a more complicated form, not to be anticipated logically on the previous level. In the same way the affirmations of Christian faith are rooted in history but add to the historical event or person an interpretation not immediately within the sphere of the historical. Another way of expressing this relationship of continuity and discontinuity is in terms of the plane geometrical axiom that from a point on a line only one perpendicular can be erected, but when the number of dimensions is increased by invoking solid geometry it becomes possible to erect another perpendicular to the previous plane at that point of intersection. The truth of the one perpendicular in plane geometry is not abrogated by the new dimension but carried to a higher level. So the Christian confession that God was in Christ does not cancel out Jesus as the first-century carpenter of Nazareth but expresses the continuity and discontinuity relationship in our knowledge of God in its sharpest form.

CHAPTER III

The Old Testament as Preparation

The position of the Bible within the Christian community has been a much-debated issue. The breakup of the organic unity of western Christendom in the Reformation period had the unfortunate result of establishing two sets of claims regarded as mutually exclusive. One claim, identified with the Roman Catholic side, held that since the Bible was in very truth the Word of God its interpretation must not be left to the isolated individual but must naturally (as the argument ran) be entrusted to the Church as the God-given institution which cannot err because of the powers of interpretation communicated to Peter and to his successors. The other claim, associated with the Reformation churches and historically productive of almost numberless sects, held that since the Bible was in very truth the Word of God its interpretation could not be entrusted to a Church which made pretensions to a divine nature but must naturally (as the argument ran) be entrusted to the responsible individual enlightened by the Holy Spirit.

What is perhaps the most significant aspect of this theological deadlock is the underlying agreement of both contenders that the

Bible was textually identical with the Word of God. The agreement extended further in that it shared a common theory of just how the Bible should be understood as the Word of God. That theory has come to be known in our day as the doctrine of infallible verbal inspiration of the writers of the holy books. It has found classic statement from the Roman Catholic side in a papal encyclical:

"All the books, which the Church receives as sacred and canonical, are written wholly and entirely, with all their parts, at the dictation of the Holy Ghost; and so far is it from being possible that any error can co-exist with inspiration, that inspiration not only is essentially incompatible with error, but excludes and rejects it as absolutely and necessarily as it is impossible that God Himself, the supreme Truth, can utter that which is not true."[1]

The same basic approach could be documented from many Protestant sources, but Hollaz is fairly representative of the extreme position:

"Scripture contains matters of history, chronology, genealogy, astronomy, physics, and politics, and although the knowledge of these may not be directly necessary to salvation, none the less they are matters of divine revelation . . . Not merely the meaning, or the things signified, but the words too, as signs of the things, are divinely inspired."[2]

This position of infallible verbal inspiration for the Bible has unfortunately been more characteristic of the Christian tradition than many Biblical scholars today care to realize. In a somewhat less sharply articulated form it was a commonplace of Jesus's day and was taken over bodily from Judaism by the early Christians. They regarded the canon of Old Testament books, whether in its more limited range in Palestinian Judaism or in its more comprehensive form at Alexandria, where the books of the Apocrypha were included, as the Word of God. When the New Testament writings

---

[1] Leo XIII, *Providentissimus Deus*, 1893.
[2] E. Brunner, *The Philosophy of Religion*, Scribner's, 1937, p. 35.

began to be grouped into a canon this Jewish doctrine of infallible verbal inspiration was uncritically applied to them also by the Church. There were, however, at least two factors that offered relief from having to accept some vengeance-filled wish of an early Old Testament character as equally the revelation of God with the sayings of Jesus, particularly the word of forgiveness from the Cross: "Father, forgive them; they know not what they do."

One of the factors was allegorism. The Old Testament, it was held, need not always be taken literally. It was an allegory of things to come. On the one hand, this approach was deeply true to the attitudes expressed by the New Testament writers, as when the author of the Epistle to the Hebrews regarded the apparatus of Old Testament sacrifice and the priesthood of Israel as a type of the higher sacrifice of Christ and of his sole high priesthood. Here the continuity between the testaments found expression in such a way that the imperfect institutions of the Old Testament were fulfilled in those of the New, which superseded them. On the other hand, this approach lost the sense that the new covenant had introduced a profound break with the old. It reduced all the writings to one grade of inspiration subject to a fanciful allegorism that could destroy the historical setting of the old. An illustration of this type of thing was the addition of section heads to the Song of Solomon, still printed in King James Bibles, thus making the lush, erotic poetry of an Israelitish connoisseur of women into a supposedly more acceptable allegory of the relation between Christ and his Church.

The second factor, less commonly acknowledged as a modifying influence, was the way in which the Bible story was preached and taught within the community of faith. Scholars are more and more seeing a direct connection between the preaching message of the early Church as it can be reconstructed from the Acts and the early New Testament epistles and the development of the early creeds. The creeds were "miniature Bibles"; that is to say, they sought to express the heart of the Christian revelation in a series of clauses mainly centered about the person and work of Christ and set in a Trinitarian confession of God as Father, Son, and Holy Spirit. That the Bible was known at all to the laity in the Middle Ages was due to the attention given to the creeds in worship and instruction and to the architectural expression of the Biblical drama in the windows and carvings of church buildings. This "core-knowledge" of the Bible was also expressed in the miracle and passion plays of the Middle Ages.

In spite of the long domination of the doctrine of infallible verbal inspiration over the Christian community it would be absurd to hold that God was without witness during this period of some eighteen hundred years. Just as God does not refuse his ministry today to the divided churches of Christendom which contradict the oneness of the Church in the New Testament documents, so God has revealed himself in the life of the community of faith in spite of the mistaken intellectual theories which the community has held about the manner of God's revelation. The perception of this kindness should save us from infatuation with what we like to believe is a wisdom of our own superior to our fathers'. It should also keep us from a "holy" complacency that would deny new insights and would rest content with a theological rationalization exposed in our day as too mechanical for the facts of Christian experience.

A quite different frame for interpreting the Bible is necessary for us today as the result of a development of some 250 years. This advance is technically called the "higher criticism," a term so suggestive of misconceptions that it should be replaced by the more immediately meaningful phrase "the historical interpretation of the Biblical documents." Far too often this movement has been described as the defensive readjustment of the Christian community to the new discoveries of science. The center of controversy has been thought to lie between the proponents of evolution and the traditionalists who would make the book of Genesis supreme as geology, astrophysics, and paleontology. Such a description has considerable truth especially as it drove some Christians to define the hitherto somewhat vaguely held doctrine of infallible verbal inspiration in increasingly exaggerated terms and in explicit disassociation from the results of scientific discovery. What such a description fails to grasp is that the root of the change is not some adjustment between the scientific world view of the ninth or fifth century before Christ and the patterns of scientific understanding today but a much more basic attitude toward the study of history and the analysis of historical sources. The scientific adjustment was from the outside, but the more fundamental historical reorientation largely resulted from new canons of historical interpretation and new discoveries in archaeology conducted by Christian scholars themselves. It was not a case of a critical historical apparatus perfected in the study of secular history suddenly being applied from the outside on the Biblical documents. Biblical scholars from within the churches forged the critical analysis of sources, the rigorous scrutiny of internal evidence, and the reconstruction of the text on the basis of philological study that has become standard procedure today in historical investigation. In other words, the present-day methodology of historians owes much more to pioneering Christian historical scholarship than is generally realized.

What is much more significant than historical primacy here or basic influence is that this association is no mere accident. It was organic to the way in which the community of faith understood that God had made himself known. The belief that God had disclosed himself and was disclosing himself in history led in the culture molded by that belief to a self-critical attitude toward the writing of history. That such an attitude could become established was due in part to the weakening of obscurantism in the churches, but that it could have been begun in the first instance, and that it took the directions it did, was due to a clear grasp on the part of the Church that history was a critical area for the determination of what man might know about God.

It is easy to understand why conservative minds in the churches felt threatened by the application of historical methods of study to the Bible. The first result seemed to be the loss of the Bible as a unified document embodying a verbally inerrant revelation of God and the substitution in its place of a collection of books, poems, and fragments of literary works extending roughly over a period of some fifteen hundred years from the war poetry typified by the Song of Deborah to the pastoral epistles of the second century after Christ. What unity was there except that of a process of history from the nomadic period of migrating Israelite clans to the period of the Pax Romana? In these turbulent years Israel lost its character as an independent nation and after a futile series of revolutions was dispersed among the nations. Had a cultural history been substituted for a revelation? Had the knowledge of God been lost in the relativism of many human histories?

Like any new movement, the "higher criticism" had, unfortunately, its devotees who deified the movement and seemed to delight in destroying the bases of faith. But in the further development of the movement these extremists were soon exposed as incompetent historians. Gradually the churches recognized the work of the Holy Spirit in what at the outset had seemed to destroy faith itself. It had been the earthen vessels and not the treasure that had been shattered. The shattering of the vessels, moreover, made it possible to appreciate the treasure in a wholly new way.

The prophets, for example, became understandable for the first time since the age of their contemporaries. Instead of mysterious sayings that required an allegorical interpretation at the mercy of the fancifulness of the expounder, these sayings were seen in the context of historical events such as the approach of Sennacherib to lay seige to Jersualem, the social injustices of eighth-century Israel just before the Assyrian invasions, the sufferings of the Babylonian exile, and the threat of apostasy to Greek culture in the Maccabean period. The prophets were analyzing current events and speaking God's words of judgment and renewal to the nation. They were supplying to the events a pattern of meaning. It is impossible to exaggerate the work of catharsis performed for the churches in the last century by such a pioneering book as George Adam Smith's on the prophets of Israel. It might be said that the tyranny of fantastic exegesis associated particularly with the book of Daniel was destroyed when Daniel was understood as an imaginative interpretation of the history of definite events in the Maccabean period and not as a sourcebook for prophecies of world destruction for nineteenth-century eccentrics.

Even more startling a discovery than the rooting of the prophets in the events of their day was the realization of a long development in the religion of Israel. Those vengeance-filled passages did not have to be explained away by allegory; they were seen as the expression of a nomadic people whose conception of God had not advanced far beyond that of a local volcano deity or a marching god of war. It was discovered that the ethical monotheism of the prophets was a late-comer. It scarcely existed before the exile of Israel to Babylon in 586 B.C. Later editors reworked earlier writings to make them more nearly expressive of the insights of the monotheistic writer of the sections of Isaiah that follow the fortieth chapter. Here again the first pioneers sometimes overstated the case for development in Israel's religion by the somewhat uncritical application of the principle of evolution. This they borrowed from the triumphant advance of biological science, but later scholars corrected their excesses by a more judicious application of the historical method itself.

These developments obviously necessitated a new understanding of the Old Testament as revelation. It could no longer be considered "the revelation" itself; it was a pointer to revelation. The pattern of continuity and discontinuity as described in Chapter 2 offered a way to understand the new dimensions of the problem. The earliest strata of Old Testament religion are continuous with the religious history of mankind. Here are the characteristic survivals of pre-animistic religion with its holy places like springs, mountains, and trees all regarded as "holy" because possessed by "mana," that nearly unanalyzable common element in all primitive religions that anthropologists have agreed to call by its Melanesian name. Here also can be discovered a continuity with primitive religions as they develop through an animistic stage with a clearer grasp on "spirits" as residing in the "mana" objects toward the stage of national religions with their polytheism and pantheons. The national religion of Israel conquered the gods or baals of the agricultural religions of the Canaanites, the Philistines, and the Phoenicians by attaching some of their attributes and functions to the clan deity of Israel.

The continuity of the religion of Israel in its earliest years with the religious expressions of paganism should not be a threatening discovery to a Christian. It simply grounds what became the distinctive witness of Christianity in the facts of everyday reality. It broadens the Christian's understanding of the way God acts in history. He takes nations and peoples where they are and leads them toward his truth. His sovereignty over history is best defined in his working with the stuff of history, not merely as some foreign invader, but as a God conscious that all men, no matter how alienated from his ways, are still men whom he created and whom he will restore by working in and through them, not simply apart from them.

To stress, however, the rootage of Israel's religion in contemporary paganism is only to emphasize one half of the mystery. What is even more remarkable than the continuity is the factor of discontinuity. Israel, while grounded in paganism and forever tempted, as the warnings of the prophets make clear, to reassociate itself with the ethnic religions, understands its mission as a chosen people. The sense of election, or of being a vocated group, is not in itself completely distinctive, for there are parallels even here in the religious development of mankind. What is distinctive, however, is the way in which this chosen people describes the relationship to God in which it believes itself to stand and the character of the God to whom it so stands in relationship. Scholars debate as to just when the concept of covenant became the basic key to Israel's religion. In all probability its explicit formulation in the documents was preceded by centuries of development from simpler forms not now discoverable for lack of evidence. In its more developed form, and it is just this ability to develop that is its special feature, the covenant was understood as a gracious relationship between God and his people Israel. God had inaugurated the relationship in his act of deliverance as he led the Israelite slaves out of Egyptian bondage. He had given specific content to it in the Mosaic Law revealed on Mt. Sinai with God's guarded appearance to Moses. It was believed that God had uniquely revealed himself in these events of the nation and later prophets would appeal to their contemporaries in the name of these saving events to remain loyal to the covenant.

What must be understood is that this covenant was not conceived as an instrument of commercial contract between two equal parties in such a way that the special protection of God was offered in exchange for the obedience of the nation. It had been the graciousness and steadfast love of God that had founded the relationship in the first place. God had taken initiative in coming to them. More and more stress came to be placed upon the need for Israel to respond in faith and in trust. Abraham became the ideal expression of this intensely personal relationship between God and his chosen people. Abraham had left the security of his birthplace and a familiar cultural environment to venture out into the unknown, confident that God would bless his seed. He believed in the promise of God.

Another aspect of this relationship that has troubled modern minds is the "jealousy" of God as portrayed in the Old Testament documents. This is just another way, the only way available at the level of development in Israel at the time, of expressing what we should call the intensely personal aspect of the relationship. In this sense "jealousy" and "wrath" are not so much unfortunate survivals of primitivism in religion as they are indispensable steps in clarifying what relationships of a personal nature mean and as preparation for a revelation of God's love that, without the patient education of Israel, might be misunderstood as sentimentality or even as an immoral love on the analogy of the sexual promiscuity practiced at the shrines of the baals. It is doubtful whether modern man, who has tended to sentimentalize the love revealed on the Cross, can understand the depth of that love without its opposite facet of the divine wrath.

In the conception of the covenant itself there thus is an expression of the continuity and discontinuity relationship. The further development of the understanding of the covenant provides another illustration of the basic pattern. The literary prophets of the eighth century and their successors are continuous with the older religion of Israel. Their historic changes in the religion are not introduced as radical departures from the tradition of the fathers. Amos and Hosea can appeal to the democratic simplicity of the nomad days to get leverage against the social injustices of a people at the peak of a class-centered prosperity in a "boom" situation between periods of warfare. The prophets attack the unethical use of the apparatus of sacrifice by describing the greater simplicity of worship in the days of wilderness wandering. "I hate, I despise your feasts, and I take no delight in your solemn assemblies. Even though you offer me your burnt offerings and cereal offerings, I will not accept them, and the peace offerings of your fatted beasts I will not look upon. Take away from me the noise of your songs; to the melody of your harps I will not listen. But let justice roll down like waters, and righteousness like an everflowing stream."[3]

The most revolutionary advance, however, in the prophets was the destruction of any "most favored nation" clause in the covenant. Amos rebukes the people for desiring the "Day of the Lord," a popular expression of the hope that God would confound and

[3] Amos 5:21-24.

destroy Israel's neighbors and establish Israel in a triumphant position. Amos opens a new dimension in religion, unthinkable on the level of a purely national covenant, when he says: "You only have I known of all the families of the earth; therefore I will punish you for all your iniquities."[4] Here the special intimacy of the covenant relation leads not to special indulgence but to special responsibility. The God of the covenant is a moral god and will punish evil in Israel as well as outside Israel. " 'Are you not like the Ethiopians to me, O people of Israel?' says the Lord. 'Did I not bring up Israel from the land of Egypt, and the Philistines from Caphtor and the Syrians from Kir?' "[5]

God is no longer only the God of the nation Israel. He is beginning to be understood as the sovereign of the nations, not by an imperialist extension of his domain by conquest, but by the ethicizing of the understanding of God. If he is the God of right anywhere he is the God of right everywhere.

It may be possible to describe common elements between Israel's early understanding of the covenant and the surrounding religions, but here in the prophetic conviction that God will punish his chosen people is a unique fact in the history of religions. It is a remarkable illustration of the pattern of continuity and discontinuity on a further level of advance. It begins to give a wholly new aspect to the idea of a chosen people. God particularizes in order to universalize. With the contributions of Amos, Hosea, and Micah the ground work is laid for the prophetic interpretation of Israel's destruction as a nation and its subsequent subjection to Babylon, Persia, Greece, Egypt, and Rome.

The national religions of the conquerors have long since perished except for a phase of Persian religion that has maintained itself among the Parsees in India. Israel, although destroyed as a nation after 597 and 586 B.C., has continued to exist as a religious community persecuted or tolerated in foreign cultures. It is prob-

4 Amos 3:2.   5 Amos 9:7.

able from the evidence of the Biblical documents and from such finds as the Elephantine Papyri that large defections to the religions of the conquerors took place, but more amazing was the power of the prophets in interpreting the destruction of the nation as God's righteous judgment on its sins. The national enemies were the rods of God's anger. With the breaking of the shell of nationality the community of Israel was free to deepen still further its understanding of the sufferings of the righteous. This is attested by the many formulations of the problem with varying answers in Job, in the rewriting of the national history to bear on this problem, in Habakkuk, in Daniel, and in the Psalms. There began to emerge a concept of a righteous remnant that became the seed plot for the Christian Church. Here was another illustration of the prevailing pattern of continuity and discontinuity.

The deepest realization of the meaning of suffering and the task of a reconstituted covenant community emerged in the Servant of the Lord poems found in the second part of Isaiah, especially in the fifty-second and fifty-third chapters. Whether the Servant is to be understood as the nation, or as a righteous remnant, or as an individual has been much debated among the historical scholars. H. Wheeler Robinson, from his profound understanding of the psychology of the Hebrews, suggests that all are possible under the Israelite view of "corporate personality." In these poems the nations perceive that the Servant has been punished for their own sins. "He was wounded for our transgressions, he was bruised for our iniquities; upon him was the chastisement that made us whole, and with his stripes we are healed."[6] Looking at the Servant they perceive that he "has poured out his soul to death" on the analogy of an offering for sin in the system of Jewish sacrifices. The Servant bore the sins of the nation and, in the totality of the offering that includes both the Servant's act and the onlookers' response, suffering is made redemptive and

[6] Isaiah 53:5.

not simply penal or destructive. Here again is an illustration of
continuity and discontinuity especially significant for the future
when Christians seek an explanation for Christ's death.

During these periods of prophetic advance and popular retro-
gression the covenant understanding received new infusions of
content. A number of legal codes can be found in the Old Testament documents like the folded strata of an exposed mountain.
One of the most famous of these codes, usually called the Deuteronomic because large sections of it are discoverable in that
book, was promulgated in 621 B.C. during the reign of the boy-
king Josiah. It consolidated in practical legislation much of the
moral advance of the earlier prophets. There is evidence that
Jeremiah supported the Deuteronomic reform in his earlier prophetic sayings but became increasingly disillusioned as to the
worth of a religion resting upon any legal code. This misgiving of
the prophet prepared the way for a new dimension of religion,
the realization that the personal nature of the covenant would
be frustrated if frozen on the level of law and that its inner principle required a new depth of inner personal relationship. Whether
from the lips of Jeremiah himself, or more probably from a later
disciple, the promise of the New Covenant would be momentous
for the future. Here a new understanding of personal relationships is revealed, a promise of a universal knowledge of God
made, and a declaration of the divine intention to forgive sin
pronounced.

"Behold, the days are coming, says the Lord, when I will make
a new covenant with the house of Israel and the house of Judah,
not like the covenant which I made with their fathers when I took
them by the hand to bring them out of the land of Egypt, my covenant which they broke, though I was their husband, says the Lord.
But this is the covenant which I will make with the house of Israel
after those days, says the Lord: I will put my law within them,
and I will write it upon their hearts; and I will be their God,
and they shall be my people. And no longer shall each man teach

his neighbor and each his brother, saying, 'Know the Lord,' for they shall all know me, from the least of them to the greatest, says the Lord; for I will forgive their iniquity, and I will remember their sin no more."[7]

This passage is a convenient summary for the chapter. It senses the inadequacy of legalism, the unsolved problem of human wrongdoing, and the need for interiorizing religion by making more responsibly personal the relation of all men to God. It suggests preparation for greater things to come. Looked at from the historical point of view, and the material of the Old Testament by its nature requires such a perspective, it is evident that there is no simple answer to the question of what revelation means in the Old Testament. Most assuredly because of the factor of development and change, with the recurring pattern of continuity and discontinuity, it will be impossible to identify the text of the writings with revelation itself. The doctrine of infallible verbal inspiration did not really grow out of the facts of the situation but was a short cut of theologians eager to have some external, oracular solution to the problem of revelation and authority for belief. The Old Testament plainly is not "the revelation." In answer to the fundamental question, "What can man know about God?" it presents no unified answer. It is a pointer to the revelation to come. The next task must be an examination of the New Testament to see whether it provides a new perspective for understanding the Old. The preparatory revelation needs fulfillment before we can grasp the true significance of the Old Testament for our knowledge of God.

[7] Jeremiah 31:31-34.

CHAPTER IV

The New Testament and the Knowledge of God

One of the difficulties in the theory of infallible verbal inspiration was that it blunted the difference in both form and content between the Old and New Testaments. On the one hand there is a religious literature arising out of the earthiness of human passions and group loyalties over a period of more than a thousand years and set in a background of the cavalcade of empires. On the other hand there are writings of the first hundred years of a new religious movement unified around one historic personality and a community responsive to him within the relatively homogenous background of the Graeco-Roman empire. The Old Testament has a human appeal all its own because of the flow of cultures it records and the varied men and women it depicts. In the New Testament all is compressed and concentrated and brought into immediate relationship with one great event. The question, "What do we know about God?" receives a definite and unambiguous answer. The key to the understanding of the Old Testament as revelation is supplied by the New Testament. Here is another example of the pattern of continuity and discontinuity:

"In many and various ways God spoke of old to our fathers by
the prophets; but in these last days he has spoken to us by a
Son . . ."[1]

The breaking of the grip of the verbal theory of inspiration has
in our day raised once more the problem of the Old Testament
for the Christian community. In the movement to accommodate
Christianity to the program of Nazism in Germany some advo-
cated the total rejection of that "Jewish" book in favor of an
"Aryan" setting for a reductionist version of Christianity. Less
crude has been the theory of some missionaries that since the New
Testament is the fulfillment of all men's religious hopes the Old
Testament could be abandoned in the cultures of the East and
their own sacred writings used as the preparation for Christ. For
all Christians the continued existence of Israel as a religious movement drawing its inspiration from the Old Testament and yet
refusing to accept what is (from the Christian perspective) its
culmination in Christ is a major challenge.

The early Church faced problems of a comparable order.
Marcion, a second-century reformer, separated the redeeming
God who had revealed his love in Christ from the Old Testament
creator God whose crudities affronted his spiritually sensitive but
unhistorical understanding. He expressed this distinction in his
repudiation of the Old Testament and in his editing of various
New Testament writings to conform to his theological approach.
Partly in opposition to this development the early Church was led
to formulate a New Testament canon. Whenever the word "scriptures" is used in the New Testament it naturally refers to the writings of the Old Testament. The realization that henceforth the
canon of the Christian Church would have its twofold form as the
scriptures of the Old and the New Covenants was the recognition
that a pattern of continuity and discontinuity was operative. The
seeds of this development were present in the teaching of Jesus,
"It has been said to you of old, but I say unto you." His statement

[1] Hebrews 1:1–2.

that the Mosaic rules on divorce written in the sacred Torah had been given for the "hardness of their hearts" and his return to the purposes of God in the creation for his special teaching on this issue was an affront to those who found security in an authoritative canon. Although the origins of the Christian community were continuous with Judaism, and Christianity was regarded by pagans of this early period as a form of Judaism, the new wine was already breaking the old skins. St. Paul battled with the conservative Jewish Christians who thought it impossible to admit gentiles into the new fellowship unless they first became Jews by circumcision and by obedience to the dietary laws. This struggle was a crisis in the reconstitution of the old Israel into the "new Israel of God," a Church universal in intent and free of racial requirements for admission.

Judaism was hostile to the new movement, and the Christian message in later New Testament documents, such as the Gospel of John, was presented in terms more readily understandable to Graeco-Roman culture, but the process of discontinuity or disassociation is always modified by specific terms of continuity. This is shown by the use of the words "covenant" and "Israel" and by the early and continuous use of the Old Testament as scripture within the new community of faith. A tempting way to dispel confusion and reduce the problem of a Christian's knowledge of God in our century to a simpler base would be to assign the Old Testament simply to a stage in the development of Christianity. It would be "there" as a body of religious literature, the study of which by specialized scholars would presumably enrich modern man's historical understanding of Christianity. But as regards the need for a layman to wrestle with this book, this burdensome chore could be eliminated. That such a proposal must be rejected suggests that something much more organic binds the Church to the Old Testament than mere historical development.

One of the most fruitful developments in historical scholarship in our day has been the rejection of a supposed contrast between the gospel of Jesus and the gospel about Jesus. The supposed antithesis was classically expressed by the great German historian, Harnack, of the past generation. He contrasted a simple moral teaching of Jesus with a religion of redemption centering in Christ, supposedly invented by the apostle Paul. The contrast has been shown to be the invention of Harnack's age and not a fact of first-century Christianity. Oscar Cullman, of the University of Basel, in his recent studies of the origins of the Christian creeds, and C. H. Dodd, of Cambridge University, in *The Apostolic Preaching and Its Development,* have increased our understanding of the historical situation. Although the Book of Acts in its finished form probably dates from about the ninth decade of the first century there is good reason for believing that the speeches attributed by the writer to the early apostles reflect the early preaching message of the Christian community. This hypothesis becomes the more credible when it is seen that the themes of this preaching are mentioned by St. Paul as part of the tradition which he had received and upon which he based his presentation of the Gospel. Furthermore, the earliest forms of what became known as the Apostles' Creed show a remarkable identity with this apostolic preaching. It may even have been the outline in the mind of the writer of the last of the gospels, the Gospel of John. A passage from St. Paul will illustrate some of these themes:

"Now I would remind you, brethren, in what terms I preached to you the gospel . . . For I delivered to you as of first importance what I also received, that Christ died for our sins in accordance with the scriptures, that he was buried, that he was raised on the third day in accordance with the scriptures, and that he appeared to Cephas, then to the twelve . . . Whether then it was I or they, so we preach and so you believed."[2]

St. Paul is plainly identifying the basic preaching which he gave to the Corinthians with the tradition he himself had received. This is an example of the *kerygma,* or basic preaching, of the ap-

[2] 1 Corinthians 15:1–5, 11.

ostolic community. The rootage of this Greek word means "a her-
ald, or a town crier, or an ambassador," and this specific message
to the non-Christian is understood in contrast to the "teaching," or
didache, which is directed to Christian communities. Since all of
St. Paul's letters are addressed to churches already in existence,
their basic content is "teaching" with the preaching message presupposed or, as in this passage, presented in summary form.

It is difficult for an age such as ours to understand both the
objectivity and the importance attributed to "preaching" in the
early community. The modern pulpit is so often simply the plat-
form for the subjective feelings of the preacher, or of his world
view, or of his most recent reading, whether from the newspaper
or the current religious book with the highest sales, that it requires
special historical imagination to appreciate a very different
"preaching" rooted in the objectivity of historical events and expressing the faith that "it pleased God by the foolishness of
preaching to save them that believe."[3] We are simply fatigued
with foolish modern preaching, not with the "foolishness" of "the
apostolic preaching."

The elements in this apostolic preaching are gathered around
the central theme: "God has visited and redeemed his people."
The first series of affirmations expresses the fulfillment of history
in terms technically called eschatological. That is to say, using the
literal meaning of *eschata* as "the final things," the past history
of Israel is now understood as having been confronted by "final
things" in the double sense that "final" means both the "temporal
end" and also "purpose." History has been given a new direction.
The age of expectation yields to the age of fulfillment. The interpretation of the new events as "according to the scriptures"
(i.e., the Old Testament) expresses the relation to past history in
a continuity now radically altered by a climactic series of events.
The writer of St. Mark's gospel introduces Jesus as preaching just
this message. "Jesus came into Galilee, preaching the gospel of

[3] 1 Corinthians 1:21. K.J.V.

God, and saying, 'The time is fulfilled, and the kingdom of God is at hand; repent, and believe in the gospel.' "[4]

The revolutionary events of Christ's life and death compose the second basic affirmation in the apostolic preaching, still preserved in the verbs of the Apostles' Creed, "suffered under Pontius Pilate, was crucified, dead, and buried." "Christ died for our sins according to the scriptures," is the way St. Paul commonly expresses it. Then the "preaching" records the resurrection of Jesus with a fullness of witness and a centrality of importance that has unfortunately been much reduced in the historic tradition of Western Christianity in both its Catholic and Protestant versions but has found eloquent expression in the liturgies of Eastern Orthodoxy. This is especially noticeable in the great Easter observances and in the many prayers for the leading of a Christian life throughout the year that invoke the power of Christ's resurrection as a never failing spring of God's action. Any objective study of the origins of Christianity cannot fail to see the importance of the resurrection of Christ for the disciples and their followers. Having fled when their master was arrested in fear and despair, if not, as in the case of Peter, in actual denial, they suddenly are met with the resurrected Christ who comes to them in spite of their failures. They see in him God's seal of approval on his earthly life. From the empirical point of view alone the transformation of hitherto defeated and fearful men into a unified community preaching with insight and power and converting their contemporaries is a historical phenomenon of the first order.

The early Christians saw the resurrection of Christ not as an isolated event but as an act of God shedding light upon the whole course of history. Moreover, Christ had not left them when the resurrection appearances ceased after a time. They believed as a further consequence of the resurrection that he had been exalted to the right hand of God from whence he would shortly return in judgment. Here past events are seen in the perspective of fu-

[4] Mark 1:14–15.

ture realities. The very course of history is being compressed in relation to a key event regarded as bearing the meaning of the whole process.

The third series of affirmations might be described as the consequences of the first two. In the light of these momentous events men are bidden to repent. They are invited to become incorporated into a fellowship of believers, the "meeting" of the new Israel of God as the fulfillment of the old Israel. In the new Church they point to the first fruits of the Spirit as already operative.

It is to the events of the life, death, resurrection, exaltation, and return of Christ that the Christian looks for the knowledge of God. Here it is believed that a history of revelation is transformed into history as revelation. What is characteristic of a Christian is not a set of intellectual convictions about the nature of God or even specific actions in conformance with the teaching or moral principles of Christ. What does characterize a Christian basically is his conviction that God has met him and will meet him in Christ and not that he has himself found God or discovered how he could be known. Of course there are intellectual convictions about God that result from this "meeting," but they are not themselves the revelation. Obviously there are new patterns of behavior and new social concerns, but they are not themselves the revelation. Moreover, this "meeting" is not a mystical experience between the self and God in isolation but an experience mediated through a historic community and mediated by history itself. There is, of course, deep religious feeling, but it is a by-product and not revelation itself. In the conviction that a series of events within time and on the plane of history, culminating in the life, death, and resurrection of Christ, is the decisive area for understanding the Christian knowledge of God, there is an empirical difference between Christianity and the other religions of mankind. This is likewise to be distinguished from all quests for God that originate

from an analysis of the structures of the world. Empirical uniqueness is not, of course, a proof of truth, but in an age which finds
relativism and subjectivism in nearly every area this is a startling
fact. It means that the drama of God's mighty acts is at the heart
of Christian concern and not, in the first instance, systems of
thought, codes of conduct, or special religious experiences.

A great Biblical dictionary, the continuing work of some of the
world's finest historical scholars, defines revelation as follows:

"Revelation is not the communication of supernatural knowledge and not the stimulation of numinous feelings. To be sure revelation can become the occasion for the growth of knowledge, and
the revelation of God is necessarily accompanied by religious feelings. But revelation does not consist of these; it is the particular
activity of God, the unveiling of his hiddenness, his giving of himself in communion."[5]

This "giving of himself in communion" is through a series of decisive historical events. Our investigation thus far has shown that,
while the Bible and the Church are indispensable to a Christian's
knowledge of God, they are not in themselves "the revelation" in
the sense that any Biblical passage or some special element in
Church life, such as a creed, are identical with revelation itself.
If we are true to the inner movement described in the Bible there
can be no question of dictated divine testimony or inerrant transcripts from writers completely freed of the relativity of their situation. They are men subject to error, conditioned by their psychological configuration, and influenced by the limited perspectives of
their country, class, and century. We must look beyond the surviv-
ing written documents, although it is only through these that we
can look at all, to what the Biblical writers are themselves pointing
to. They point to a series of events on the plane of history as the
locus for God's revelation. Our attention must increasingly be cen-

[5] Kittel, *Theologisches Woerterbuch zum Neuen Testament,* Vol.
III, p. 575.

tered on that history as decisive for the Christian knowledge of God.

But the more this is done the more puzzling becomes the problem of history itself. Quite obviously history is an ambiguous word: it may be used to indicate a series of events or it may be used to describe the narration in a special way of a series of events. For example, Roman historiographers who might have stood in the crowd when Jesus was crucified would agree with some of the verbs of the apostolic preaching, such as "was crucified under Pontius Pilate" and "dead and buried." What they would not agree to would be the interpretation, "Christ died for our sins according to the scriptures." Yet it is just this special interpretation placed upon the event that gives it its decisive meaning for the Christian. Is there then a "sacred history" as against a "secular history," making for the moment the perhaps quite unwarranted assumption that the Roman historians would represent the latter type? There are Christian theologies in our day that base their approach on *Heilsgeschichte,* or "sacred history," but their inadequacy is that, while they achieve simplicity, they do so at the expense of serious misconception. The Living God who is described in the Biblical documents is presented in the later prophets as the Lord of all history, not of some portion of it hermetically sealed off from the rest of what would then be left as "secular" history. The problem of God's relation, if any, to "secular" history would still remain. The area of redemption would be reserved for the "sacred" segment. The great prophets of the Old Testament and certainly the writers of the New Testament have painted on a much bolder canvas.

Just as God chose to reveal himself by working *within* Israel's primitive life and not simply unrelatedly *from without,* so the evidence points to a similar relationship between the revelatory events and history itself. The crossing of the Red Sea, the threat of foreign invasion from Egypt, Assyria, or Babylon, the exile, the return to Palestine in the reign of Cyrus—these are events woven warp and woof into the pattern of the regional history of the Near East over a thousand years. The death of Christ presumably appeared in the official chronicles of Pilate's governorship along with the names of other malefactors, insurrectionists, and troublers of the Roman peace. These are not events done in a corner in the dark. The Christian claims to see in them a communication of meaning for the whole of history. The mystery as to just why these events are singled out from many other events is not adequately described as a contrast between "sacred" and "secular" history. It is not so much then in the "facticity" of the event that the problem is to be centered but in varying interpretations that are placed upon the same event.

This means that history itself is a highly complicated subject. Even those who have defined it contemptuously as "just one damn thing after another" testify by the adjective to some interpretation that presupposes a whole philosophy of life. It was a mistake when some historians of the past century, overwhelmed by the success of chemistry and physics in apparently simplifying matter by an analysis of it into discreet atoms, began to interpret history as a series of "atomic" facts, that is to say, as events on the analogy of separate particles in motion. Even the most prosaic chronicler is forced to select his events from the inexhaustible manifold of experience. He could not possibly record all the events of a lifetime, let alone the story of the centuries. Every selection of events presupposes some values which are not immediately given with the stuff of history. The virtue of the period of "scientific" history was to teach reverence for the primary documents and for the "happenness" of events. Its shortcoming was in not facing up to the whole problem of history as an interpretive story and in not being critical enough about its own presuppositions when it judged too severely the values and interpretations of others.

To say then that the Christian knows God as revealing himself in history does not mean that an archaeological expedition might dig him up in Palestine. That is the fallacy of historicism. For history is much more than a mere chronicle of past doings, and it is just in this deeper dimension that Christian faith sees history as the revelation of God. Our concern with man's knowledge of God requires us now to ask what history really is.

CHAPTER V

Revelation and History

The events which the Christian sees as providing knowledge about God occur as the history first of the people of Israel, then of the Church, or the "new Israel of God." From an external point of view these events are part of the common history of mankind—the wanderings of peoples in a heroic age, the battles by which a people establishes itself in what becomes a homeland, the subsequent struggle to defend that homeland against foreign invasion, the cultural opposition to neighboring peoples, yet borrowing from them, military defeat, the exile of the nation, and its subsequent restoration as a vassal kingdom under new powers. Whether these events are those of ancient Israel or modern Poland or Korea, they occur again and again in the course of history.

What distinguishes the particular series associated with Israel from any other series is that a special interpretation is placed upon these events, an interpretation which the Christian understands as shedding meaning upon any recurrence of the series or parts of the series, whether in Poland, America, or elsewhere. This is not to suggest that there is a mechanical necessity behind this pattern of events. The power of prediction in the prophets is qualified by a recognition that the future is still open. Men may repent and thereby release new powers to change a deadlock between nations or a breakdown between classes of competing interests within a nation. The probabilities, however, are that men will not repent. The rise and the fall of empires develops a pattern not of pre-ordained necessity but of human persistence in evil-doing. It is the freely willed determinism of sin, not divine decree, nor fate, that is our problem.

The special interpretation of the events found in the narratives about Israel in the Bible is part of the history itself and has entered into the stream of history, further influencing and directing its course. While there may be something quite unique in the contents of this interpretation, it is not at all unique that interpretations of events should influence history itself. Hitler's conviction that modern Germany was the ordained instrument of the New Order to realize the superiority of the Aryan stock altered the history of contemporary Europe. The interpretation of history written in the British Museum by a German exile and recluse is still shaking the very foundations of our world in a rising tide of Marxist activity. Ideas about history can become potent forces in history when they are embodied in persons and communities.

There is no writing of history which is not also an interpretation of history. In this sense the writing of history is less to be compared with science than with art. Often when the "scientific" history of a series of events is written it is not particularly illuminating. It may even fail to understand subsequent series of events because it was just the special interpretation placed upon the early events, an interpretation not easily caught within the scientific historian's net of inscriptions, earliest sources, environmental determination, cultural, religious, and psychological conditioning, that influenced the course of subsequent history itself.

The "facts" about the Plymouth Colony of 1620 are readily discoverable from the documents and digging. A mixed group of exiles, some determined to break with their native land in order to worship God as their consciences directed, others discontented with economic and social restrictions in the English society of that period and eager to break new ground in a wilderness colony, were largely financed by a company with the hope of profit on risk capital. Many recent histories of the Pilgrims have emphasized simply the economic factors in this commercial enterprise, never very successful financially or impressive sociologically in terms of the numbers of people involved. Partly these economic histories were a needed corrective to earlier ones which stressed the religious factor as the sole motivation in strange contradiction to the known facts of human behavior. Partly these "scientific" histories were needed to correct quite fanciful myths about the Pilgrims which saw in them the foundation of representative democracy and even of the free enterprise system that distinguished nineteenth-century economic expansion. On the other hand, these "scientific" histories were not quite "scientific" enough. They failed to appreciate that man has a more complex motivation than economic drive and that, in spite of the numerical insignificance of the Plymouth Colony and its final absorption into the stronger Massachusetts Bay Colony, it molded subsequent history not primarily as "facts" analyzable in scientific terms but as a special interpretation of history and, as such, organically one with and inseparable from the stream of events.

"The place of the Pilgrim Fathers in American history can best be stated by a paradox. Of slight importance in their own time, they are of great and increasing significance in our time, through the influence of their story on American folklore and tradition. And the key to that story, the vital factor in this little group, is the faith in God that exalted them and their small enterprise to something of lasting value and enduring interest."[1]

The clue to understanding the element of interpretation in all writing of history is provided by the words "lasting value" and "enduring interest." While the play of social, economic, and cul-

[1] Samuel Eliot Morison, *By Land and By Sea*, Knopf, 1953, p. 234.

tural factors must never be neglected, the really significant thing about history is that it is made by persons loyal to sets of values who mold and are molded in turn by communities of persons also with distinctive scales of values. The actions of such individuals and the responses of such groups must possess an "enduring interest" for subsequent generations in order that they should be of concern for historians. Otherwise the events would have been forgotten.

The problem of history is therefore given a quite false simplicity when it is analyzed into supposed "facts" accessible to scientific determination apart from interpretations placed upon these "facts." The historian deals more with portraits than with candid camera shots. He must always be sensitive to what lies behind the portrait and seek to set out "what occurred" to the eyes of a contemporary onlooker. Therefore the "scientific" interpretations of Biblical history, sometimes extremely prosaic, play an important role. They recall the historian to the basic rootage of all history in political, economic, and sociological realities and prevent fanciful interpretations that in their devotion to certain values may blind the later observer to the complex framework in which the events originally took place. This regulative function is only, however, part of the historian's task. When the Christian points to the events of Old Testament history as giving us knowledge about God he is referring primarily to the element of interpretation which we have seen to be inseparably bound up with the course of history itself and not merely a readily detachable philosophy to be attributed solely to the eccentricities or predilections of writers of later periods.

The major difference then between the interpretation which Isaiah placed upon current events and that placed upon them by most of his own contemporaries was that for him they had a meaning in terms of which he saw God active in history in a special way. That history should itself be regarded as a meaningful process is a momentous conviction, not a self-evident inference from experience. The fact that this conviction is widespread among our contemporaries is the cultural deposit in the West of the Jewish-Christian attitude toward history as a meaningful disclosure of God's purposes. Most of our contemporaries, even though they may have rejected a distinctively religious meaning, are prepared to ask for meaning in history. The seeming naturalness of this demand or question is by no means obvious when the background is widened to include cultures outside of the Jewish-Christian heritage. For most of the peoples of Asia in their historic religions and philosophies, history is regarded as a chain of phenomenal happenings without basic reality. History, in short, is *Maya;* it belongs to the realm of the illusory and must not be considered a serious area where meaning might be revealed. This lack of interest in the historical which characterizes most Eastern religions and philosophies is paralleled by the typical attitude of Greek culture to history. What meaning there was in history for the Greek was to be discovered in the cyclic rise and fall of city-states and empires. History, in other words, was swallowed up by nature, and the calendar of the seasons became the theme for understanding the movement of history. Spengler's theory of the youth, maturity, and senescence of cultures is a modern variant on the Greek theme.

It is significant that, when the Renaissance deliberately sought to rehabilitate the classic view of man, it did so on the basis not of a return to the classic view of history as essentially meaningless recurrence but on the basis of a secularized version of Christian meaning. It gradually established "progress" as the unfolding of man's infinite capacity for development as the substitute for the view that God will judge the nations and in his own good time inaugurate his Kingdom. It could not bring itself to rehabilitate the classical view of history as essentially meaningless. Renaissance dependence upon the Biblical tradition of a meaningful history is nowhere more evident than in its morale, which is exultant and confident as against the profound melancholy of Greek culture on the meaning of life. Aristotle remarked that it were better for man had he not been born. The ethics of classical culture, whether in its hedonistic or naturalistic phases, is essentially instruction on how to bail and keep the lifeboat temporarily afloat, knowing full well that it is destined for destruction in the seas of meaninglessness.

Even Marxism, with its official hostility to the Western religious heritage, betrays itself as a child of that culture by its confidence that history is a meaningful process. Economic determinism replaces divine providence, the party becomes the Church, and the revolutionary establishment of the dictatorship of the proletariat substitutes for God's inauguration of the Kingdom. But meaning there must be!

The continuing inheritance of expecting meaning in history is sometimes disclosed in amusing absent-mindedness on the part of historians whose official method they should wish to call "scientific." H. A. L. Fisher sets forth his verbal philosophy early in his great study of European history:

"One intellectual excitement has, however, been denied me. Men wiser and more learned than I have discovered in history a plot, a rhythm, a pre-determined pattern. These harmonies are concealed from me."[2]

And yet, as his history proceeds, it is clear that it leads up to the parliamentary democracy of nineteenth-century liberalism in accordance with a view of progress which he assumes throughout and explicitly refers to a few lines after the earlier disclaimer of meaning: "The fact of progress is written plain and large on the page of history."[3]

The quarrels between moral perfectionists, Marxists, and democratic utopians, while bitter and filled with significance for what our future history will be and perhaps for what will be left of the natural world now that historical man possesses the key to atomic energy, are seen as family quarrels beside the assertion of

[2] H. A. L. Fisher, *The History of Europe*, Mifflin, 1935, p. vii.
[3] Ibid., p. vii.

most non-Western cultures that history is without essential meaning. The breath-taking originality of the prophets in seeing history meaningfully as God's disclosure has provided even some of the faith's most resolute adversaries with their structures of meaning and expression.

In addition to the dimension of meaning or interpretation history is usually history for some special group of persons living in a community. There are civilizations long since dead which are now in process of having histories of a limited type written about them on the basis of archaeological research and the deciphering of ancient documents or inscriptions newly brought to light. Few men will passionately contest the interpretation which the modern historian will place upon his limited evidence. Yet as soon as these dead civilizations are made raw material for some comprehensive philosophy of history, such as Toynbee undertakes with his analysis of some twenty-one civilizations, the subject which aroused little interest as a scholarly monograph now becomes a matter of concern for us. What happened to the Aztecs, the Minoans, the Indus Civilization suddenly becomes controversial when it is interpreted as throwing light upon our situation and the probabilities of our future history. There is probably no segment of human history so completely dead that it is not capable of becoming a contemporary bone of contention. Because history is concerned with values, and man is a creature who cherishes values, any new interpretation of why Rome fell has the potentiality of arousing conflict and usually does.

This communal devotion to value and meaning is intensified when we are looking back at events belonging to the series of which we are now a part and which find their interpretation in a living community. The one unifying and continuous thread amid the complexity of the Biblical documents and their tangled historical configurations is that it is at base the history of a community of faith. It is the story of God's revelation to a continuing "people of God" who stretch from Abraham to the most recently founded

Christian churches in Sumatra. All communities of faith understand their history from within, from participation rather than from outside observation.

American history means something different for an American from what it does for a Frenchman even though the latter may express the most delicate sympathy. Likewise no American, even with the best scholarship or insight, can really see French history as a native Frenchman does. The foreigner may actually see things that are not immediately obvious to the American in his history as De Tocqueville did in the 1830s and Bryce did in the expansionism of the Cleveland era. In this sense the outsider may contribute immeasurably to a critical understanding of American history. Yet it is just this other dimension of history as experienced within a community of value that is capable of exciting strong positive and negative responses. This latter is existential or experienced history. It is to the documents of such history that we must turn for a revelation of meaning.

"The American way of life" is a phrase that expresses a communal apprehension of value. While this phrase is regularly perverted by political opportunists and can become an expression of self-idolatry with stultifying historical consequences, yet the standard of what is "American" or "un-American" answers to something deep within the American spirit. The Pilgrim fathers, the Boston Tea Party, Bunker Hill, Valley Forge, the Alamo, and Abraham Lincoln are all memories evoked by that phrase. The "Gettysburg Address" was itself an interpretation of history that in turn entered into and influenced the course of history. An analysis of it will show those feelings of reverent memory and group loyalty that become for every American generation a new challenge to action. Lincoln does not state that the nation was founded in 1776 although that is the "scientific" fact. "Our fathers" evokes a response similar to "our forefather Abraham." This is *our* story. Even the "fourscore and seven years ago" draws its force not alone from the literary affinities it suggests with King James English and with Shakespeare but somehow humanizes that time span; it is our time, the time of our history. It is within the lifetime of a man. Even the act of founding the country receives deeper personalization by verbs which compare the event to the birth of a child and presuppose the Christian rite of baptism or dedication: ". , . brought forth on this continent a new nation, conceived in liberty and dedicated to the proposition . . ." All of this makes the phrasing of the proposition extremely dramatic and intimate: ". . . that all men are created equal." The historic document of the Declaration of Independence gains new luster in these short sentences.

But not all have eyes to see; that is to say, not all see these events with American eyes. With external objectivity the English historian writing in the Cambridge Modern History comments:

"If we regard the Declaration as the assertion of an abstract political theory, criticism and condemnation are easy. It sets out with a general proposition so vague as to be practically useless. The doctrine of the equality of men, unless it be qualified and conditioned by full reference to special circumstance, is either a barren truism or a delusion."[4]

But let us return to the document that reveals "the American way" and to its author who regarded the founding fathers as our fathers when they committed treason against their lawful sovereign in the name of the liberties of Englishmen. The address speaks of the consecration of a cemetery for the dead, ironically mistaken in its prediction that "the world will little note nor long remember what we say here, but it can never forget what they did here." The deed has been chiefly remembered because of the word and would never have been as meaningful without it. In the true style of the prophets of Israel who, after recalling God's mighty acts, challenge their hearers to respond by the appropriate behavior, Lincoln urges "us, the living," to dedicate ourselves to the unfinished task of the heroes "that this nation, under God, shall

[4] *Cambridge Modern History*, Macmillan, 1903, Vol. 7, p. 174. Quoted by Richard Niebuhr in *The Meaning of Revelation*.

have a new birth of freedom; and that government of the people, by the people, for the people, shall not perish from the earth." Here the values of the Declaration are given more profound depth than in their original form and a promise and a criterion of judgment given to Americans for interpreting the problems of our future.

It is history of this caliber that we find in the Bible and in the Church, the inner history of a community of faith. For faith is that response to value revealed which characterizes the "Gettysburg Address." In seeking to find God's revelation in the history of the community of faith we are not pursuing some esoteric method but looking into just the area of life where man realizes that the most important things are revealed. National history is the remembrance of events significant for the life of national communities. The history of Israel and the Church is the remembrance of events of crucial importance and significance for all men everywhere. These events are the common happenings of everyday life and the life of nations. What is unique here is that the particular interpretation placed upon these events gives clues to universal meaning behind and beyond the process itself. The insight of the prophets into their times pierces through the foreground of events to the perspective from which the canvas has been painted. That point is God's purposes for the world particularized and concentrated in events which are not very remarkable, taken solely by themselves or looked at from the observer's point of view, rather than from the participant's decisions in a community of response. The Assyrian threat to Jerusalem, the Babylonian capture and enslavement of Jerusalem, the reconstitution of the nation under Cyrus—these events are not in themselves very remarkable. What is remarkable is that the prophets see the Living God of history as judging nations for their social injustice and their arrogant foreign policies. This judgment is achieved within history by the processes of history itself. Evil behavior boomerangs upon those who exchange good for the expedient or trust in power realities apart from moral decisions. The judgment is accomplished by the breakdown of morale in a nation, rendering it easy prey to an enemy, or by the blinding of vision that accompanies a false estimate of a nation's strength and security. The judgments of God are not *deus ex machina* invasions but are discernible only to the eyes of faith in such manner that a "scientific" historian might explain the course of events as interrelated chains of political, economic, or sociological causation. The prophets, however, see more than the judgments of God. They see the Living God mercifully present in history. That is to say, the judgments of God are also expressions of loving concern. No judgment is so negative or overwhelming that it cannot provide an opportunity for the renewal of the nation or for the renewal of a remnant within the nation that can see and accept the judgment creatively. The hope of Ezekiel that the Spirit of the Lord will breathe again the breath of life into the very dry bones of the dead nation, the promise of a return to Palestine across a desert that will blossom as the rose, all these are expressions of renewal. They might also be explained by the "scientific" historian as a shift in the foreign policy of a new world power eager to expand its domain by attaching to itself the loyalty of peoples recently subjected to the tyranny of its predecessor.

This common framework of prophetic interpretation reveals very definite information about God. It reveals the God who takes a personal interest in the history of Israel. This God is not a power of nature or a process remote from man. He is the "Living God," standing in covenantal relationship to his chosen people. He is the God of the moral order whose holy justice plays no favorites in history. His chosen people will be punished exactly as any other nation for its sins. He is the God of mercy whose punishment of the nations and of men is not an end in itself but an opportunity for a creative renewal and advance. The justice and mercy of God are not expressions of a conflict within God between two opposite motivations but the revelation of a living God whose way of reconciling what to man may seem contradictory is partly, but not fully, revealed in the Old Testament. It awaits the decisive revelation of the Cross under the New Covenant.

In locating the center of God's revelation in the prophetic interpretation of history an obvious difficulty arises. The Bible presents more than the historical events of Israel or of the new Israel of God. It sets this history in a suprahistorical frame of reference. The Bible begins with an account of the Creation of the world, with the Fall of mankind in Adam, with a great judgment upon mankind in the Noachian flood, and with the scattering and confusion of the nations for idolatrous pretensions in the Tower of Babel. It closes with a picture of world judgment when Christ returns in glory and the nations and peoples stand before the Great Judge.

No prophet obviously participated in the events of Creation and the Fall, nor could he be present at the Last Judgment, which must still occur. The center of attention here, moreover, is not Israel but all the world. How is this suprahistorical framework in which the history of the people of God is narrated to be explained?

The answer must be obvious. The prophetic insight into Israelite history is here universalized in the dimensions of time and space. The writers of the early chapters of Genesis are reworking ancient folklore about origins, early Babylonian and Canaanite myths of creation, to make them expressive on a world canvas of the special insights of the prophetic interpretation of history. These are suprahistorical "acts" of judgment and renewal. God's revelation of himself to the prophets in the contemporaneity of their times and in the particularity of a chosen nation is meant to be of universal human significance. The particularization and concentration upon Israel which forms the major bulk of the narrative is revealed as educative and missionary rather than ultimately exclusive. God chooses *some* men in order to save *all* men.

Most nations have myths about their origins and their destinies, dreams either of a future or a past golden age. Plato uses myth when he wishes to teach deep truths about the soul which are only poorly expressed in the rational transcripts of conventional philosophy. His myths illuminate the eternal world of the forms and the timeless values, but to the depreciation of the visible temporal world. The Biblical "myths" of Creation, Fall, and the Last Judgment deal admittedly with "events" that transcend ordinary history, but not in an unhistorical interest. With its point of reference securely anchored in the stuff of history the literary form of the myth is used in the Bible as a pointer to the Living God who is the beginning and the end of all things. Here is another unusual example of continuity of a literary type and of a common folklore interest, but also of a radical discontinuity that makes the Biblical understanding of time quite different from that in Greek culture.

The story of the scattering of the nations and the confounding of their tongues in the Tower of Babel is followed by the call of Abraham out from among the nations. This account of the election of Abraham has the same structure as the call of Moses and the deliverance of the children of Israel from Egyptian bondage with the institution of the Covenant at Sinai. Much of this early material probably belongs to legend but also illustrates how profoundly the revelatory insights of the prophets have shaped the oral traditions of the nation. Here the "Word of God" which came to the prophets is beginning to be understood as a Word addressed to all men and nations. "In the beginning was the Word, and the Word was with God, and the Word was God."[5]

The Biblical writers, as must now be evident from the last three chapters, understand that history is the locus for God's self-revelation. The prophets see the Living God of Judgment and Grace present in the historic challenges which come to the nation. A faith grounded in the reality of God's presence and purpose in contemporary responsibilities and inescapable decisions grows in depth until the particularism of a chosen people and a national covenant is transformed into a universal mission and into a covenant of faith, not of birth. The God of Israel's present concern is

[5] John 1:1.

increasingly understood as the God of the Beginning and the End.
Thought about Creation and Eschatology did not spring from a
speculative interest in temporal origins or in temporal endings but
arose as a corollary or consequence of the religious concern with
present fellowship with God. Even the suprahistorical setting of
the Biblical narrative by its constitutive principles testifies to the
centrality of history as the primary locus for man's understanding
of God. This revelation through history cannot be grasped if certain events are analyzed simply from an external point of view.
These events must be looked at from a community that has experienced them and lives in memory of the values which it has
found in the events.

Another example of the dominating interest in the historical
sphere as the primary area of God's self-disclosure is the way in
which the Old Testament writers see God revealed in nature,
either in its regular sequences of beauty and order or in miraculous
change. They find him there as its Creator and Sustainer by the
deepening of their faith that he has bound himself to the nation
in a historical covenant relationship. There is a long struggle between the God of Israel as the God of the invading nomad clans
and the baals of the agricultural religions of the more technically
advanced peoples living within Palestine. The triumph of Israel
is accompanied by the extension of Israel's God over the realm of
nature, not merely by conquest, but by the fundamental reinterpretation of nature in a historical interest. As their way of
life became more centered around agriculture we can see evi-
dences of defections on the part of the Israelites to the nature
deities of the surrounding nations. But the prophets deepened the
sphere of Israel's God to include man's present needs by relating
the God of the Covenant to their newer concerns. The nations
surrounding Israel never progressed beyond the stage of religions
of nature. Because of the creative interpretation of the prophets,
Israel came to recognize God as the Creator and Sustainer of the
natural world as a deepening of their previous experience of him

as the God of their history who had bound himself to his nation. Thus "nature" is understood religiously from the point of view of "history."

Our abstract words "history" and "nature" are apt to suggest to us almost independent fields which we may then possibly relate to God's self-disclosure. There were no such "middle neutralities" to the Hebrew mind. H. Wheeler Robinson comments on the lack of any Hebrew word for "nature," saying that the Hebrew would have used "God." The world was directly transparent to God. This marvelous plasticity of nature to the living God is clearest in the pictures of the future painted by the prophets. In the new age nature will be marvelously transformed. The desert will blossom as the rose, the rough places will be made plain, and predatory animals will lose their viciousness as lions lie down with lambs and a little child leads them. In the New Testament book of Revelation there is the vision of new heavens and a new earth with no more sea. In emphasizing "history" as the primary field of God's revelation we must not imply that "nature" is excluded. It is excluded as the primary field but included within "history" as part of the Living God's revelation to his creatures. The contrast between "history" and "nature" is the result of our own development, not of any original separation as distinct spheres in the Hebrew mind.

Modern man in the West, as has been developed in an earlier chapter, generally intuits nature religiously with eyes of faith influenced by his historical tradition. This can be illustrated by an incident from a college walking tour. Some American Christian students, hiking with a Christian Japanese friend, stopped on a mountain trail to admire a sunset. The silence was broken by the Japanese, who said uncomfortably: "Such an experience is deeply threatening for one raised in the Shinto tradition who has learned as a Christian to see God revealed primarily in people and in history." The American boys, products of a cultural tradition that had emphasized God as the Creator and Sustainer of nature but defined primarily as personal and loving in a historical revelation, felt no threat in the sunset. It was for them even sacramental of God's presence, whereas the residual pull of a nature religion, even upon one who had consciously changed his religious orientation, made the sunset a threat. Here clearly is the distinction between nature viewed from the historical perspective and nature regarded by itself as the primary area of divine disclosure.

Having located God's revelation in history, it is important not to confuse this locus with revelation itself. There remains a dimension in this problem beyond the events themselves. This indispensable factor is the faith engendered, to be sure, only by the special events as stimuli but grounded much more deeply in the meeting of God and men. Revelation is not simply history. God cannot be dug up in Palestine. Historicism, whether in the form of scholarly investigation that is oriented in an antiquarian direction without raising questions of contemporary meaning, or in the form of archaism by which churches have bound themselves to a "past deposit of revelation" with a loss of the experience of the Living God in the present, is in both forms a corruption of the Biblical understanding of revelation. It isolates only the first element in the provisional formula for revelation previously described as event plus a believing interpretation of the event. It remains to discuss more fully the second element, the believing interpretation, as that faith is inextricably related to the historical locus. It may be discovered that such vital integration of event and believing interpretation will lead to a reformulation of the provisional definition and that it will stress the person of Christ as the illuminative key to history as the locus of revelation. If such be the case, there will be a further illustration of the pattern of continuity and discontinuity within the development from our tentative definition of revelation to its climax and crown in Jesus Christ.

CHAPTER VI

Revelation and Faith

The series of revelatory events in Israel culminating in the drama of Christ's life, death, and resurrection is the public or communal revelation of the Bible. It is just this public and open character which distinguishes what the Bible means by revelation from numberless esoteric cults that lead to secret wisdom and issue in anarchic individualism. The public character of the historical events frees the Biblical revelation from individualistic subjectivism.

This public revelation, however, requires as its necessary complement a private revelation. Otherwise it would never gain credence for itself. It would remain "out there" as an unappropriated tradition. Luther has said that just as everyone must do his own dying so everyone must do his own believing. No one can believe for us. The Biblical understanding of revelation requires that it be personally appropriated and assimilated. Scholastic theories of an "implicit faith" in the authority of the holy community are at best questionable pedagogical aids. They are more often corruptions and substitutes for individual responsibility. This twofold nature of public and private revelation, of tradition and

personal appropriation, of group and individual experience, raises
the question of the relation of the individual to the group.

The political and economic history of our times is embroiled over
this problem. The American of today inherited a theory of rugged
individualism which was largely the result of pioneering in a virgin
continent. He is beginning to discover that his simple creed inherited from the past fails to meet the domestic and international
power complexes of the twentieth century. The communists, on
the other hand, in a despairing reaction from bourgeois individualism, have swallowed the person in the maw of the state. Their
practice of glorifying the heroes of the revolution and the martyrs
of abortive revolutions, however, strangely belies the dogmatism of
their theory. Our confusion is further expressed in two conflicting
tendencies. In general, studies in social philosophy tend to exaggerate the creative role of groups, whereas many of our psychological interpretations of man underrate the formative factors of the
group on the individual. The self-made man is an illusion possible
only to nineteenth-century American expansionism. We are literally given our lives by our families, our friends, our business associates, and by the traditions of value in church, party, lodge, and
nation.

Arnold Toynbee has illuminated the problem of the individual
and society in his comprehensive survey of world history. He con-
cludes that a society "is a relation between individuals; and this
relation of theirs consists in the coincidence of their individual
fields of action; and this coincidence combines the individual fields
into a common ground; and this common ground is what we call
a society." Then follows the important observation that "a field
of action . . . cannot be a source of action . . . The source of
social action cannot be the society, but can only be each or some
or one of the individuals whose fields of action constitute a society
on the ground where they coincide."[1]

[1] Arnold J. Toynbee, *A Study of History,* Oxford, 1945, Vol. III,
p. 230.

The Biblical understanding of revelation is one in which public and private experience are interpreted as necessarily complementary rather than antagonistic aspects. This duality can be illustrated by the autobiographies of the Hebrew prophets. Nothing reads more like an authentic expression of individual religious experience than the call of the prophet Isaiah.[2] His experience comes "in the year that King Uzziah died" with all the perplexing problems of an interregnum in a Near Eastern principality. The uncertainties of his country's history in a time of crisis are the background for an intensely personal experience: "I saw the Lord sitting upon a throne." The picture of the majesty of the heavenly court and the holiness of the Lord expresses no mere passive acceptance of a religious tradition but the actual experience of meeting between God and man. The prophet's confession of individual and social guilt follows this vision of the Righteous Lord. "Woe is me! For I am lost; for I am a man of unclean lips, and I dwell in the midst of a people of unclean lips; for my eyes have seen the King, the Lord of hosts!" Then follows an act, somewhat naïve and primitive, that announces God's forgiveness of sins by his burning out of guilt as the fiery coal touches the lips of the prophet in his vision. This theme will be deepened and moralized until the Son of God dies for the sins of all men on the Cross. Immediately after the experience of cleansing comes the call: "Whom shall I send, and who will go for us?" The prophet, true to the Biblical experience of revelation as no mere meeting for enjoyment or ecstasy, but as a challenge to action and to mission, replies: "Here I am! Send me."

The personal element in his experience is primary. We are not dealing with an "implicit faith" but with a lively response that involves the whole person. What is still more significant then is that this individual experience simply reflects the whole social and historical revelation of the Bible. The Living God of history, holy and righteous, confronts man in his historic responsibilities. This Living

[2] Isaiah 6.

God pronounces judgment on sin and offers forgiveness or renewal of relationship. Man is sent to his fellows to witness to this Living God. In other words, the whole public Old Testament pattern of revelation is the active presupposition and formative structure for this intensely individual experience.

The need for a personal appropriation in the experience of revelation finds its parallel in the analysis made of the American way of life in a previous chapter. (What follows applies to the immigrant to any new country, such as Australia or Israel, of course.) The immigrant to this country must pass through a process, interestingly described as "naturalization." The oath which the foreigner swears to support the Constitution is but the outward and visible sign of a whole lifelong process of assimilating his new nation's history and values. He must somehow come to acknowledge the Pilgrims as "his fathers," do penance for their religious bigotry and for racism, rejoice in Bunker Hill as "his battle," and somehow cherish both Lee and Lincoln as great Americans. Perhaps his most difficult task will be to appropriate the true Americanism of the fathers and maintain at the same time a critical attitude to a false "Americanism" sponsored by political interest groups and some "patriotic" societies. Far from being a mere intellectual education or an exercise in controlled imitation, this type of participation in the nation's heritage involves moral judgments and decisions. He must be ready to defend this national heritage and tradition of values if the nation is challenged from without or from within.

The need for a faith response before the historical locus of revelation is transmuted into the actuality of personal revelation can be illustrated by a lyrical outburst in Professor Morison's history of the era of the clipper ships. After a section of "ordinary" history that contains biographical sketches of the ship designers, plans of the clippers, and quite prosaic details of tonnage and financial backing occurs this "participated in" history, in which the *Flying Cloud* is addressed as a living being and all its relics invested with sacramental significance. This is not "objective" history; it is a much deeper and more meaningful history. It is the testimony of a faith.

"O Flying Cloud, what eulogy and admiration you had in your lifetime; what joyous hours have been spent by armchair sailors, gloating over your records and the spare journals of your voyages; what delight is given today even by models, prints, and paintings, imperfect images of you in your splendor, as you logged your eighteen knots in the trade winds, studding sails set aloft and alow; or as you fought and battled to windward off Cape Horn, topgallant masts housed and stripped to double-reefed topsails! Donald McKay built faster clippers and larger clippers; but for general all-round excellence you were his masterpiece."[3]

The position of the twentieth-century Christian today is not radically different from that of Isaiah in the eighth century before Christ in terms of the need for appropriating his religious tradition. The Christian faith is what its name implies; it is a faith. Peter answered the direct question, "Who do you say that I am?" with a confession of faith that was further underscored as faith, not sight, nor reason, etc., in the reply: "Blessed are you. For flesh and blood has not revealed this to you, but my Father who is in heaven." So today as in the New Testament period, "No one can say Jesus is Lord except by the Holy Spirit." That is to say, faith is man's openness to God that makes it possible for man to receive God's revelation. It is a word that denotes an attitude of openness and yet concern on the part of man; it is also a word that expresses the God-given quality of revelation. The two perspectives are not contrary but express the reality of revelation as appropriated by the person. This means also that revelation is understood in its own light. God the Holy Spirit expresses the developed Christian conviction that God himself must be his own witness. The Holy Spirit is "God active in human life" in pointing the individual living in his community of faith to the great reve-

[3] S. E. Morison, *By Land and By Sea*, p. 44.

latory events that are at the foundation of faith and that are continuously being appropriated anew in the worship and witness of
the community. To state that revelation can be understood only in
its own light sounds like a theological trick either to short-circuit
a fundamental analysis or to make irrationality more palatable.
It is neither of these. There are some experiences so basic in life
that they need to be presupposed in order to be intelligible as
experiences. For example, light can only be experienced in terms
of light. To say that revelation is only meaningful in terms of its
self-authenticating quality is simply to state the only meaningful
way in which it can be discussed. The acceptance of the Christian
revelation as a faith is not in itself an irrational act. It may be the
only way of expressing a relationship in the field of knowing that
when accepted is seen to disclose an ultimate rationality.

"Faith . . . precedes its own rational vindication, not only as a
matter of usual experience, but as a matter of inherent necessity.
But that does not mean that it is itself irrational; it only means
that it is itself the illumination whereby its rational grounds are
discovered."[4]

The insistence upon the element of personal appropriation in
the Biblical understanding of revelation, and the conviction that
God the Holy Spirit must work within our hearts and minds before
we can be vitally responsive to the faith which is mediated to us
by the community, direct attention to another facet of the problem. The historical events which have been described are the locus
of revelation and not revelation itself. Historicism is just as much
a perversion of the Christian faith as Gnosticism is in its denial
of the historical element. The remembered events of salvation,
although the indispensable precondition, are but the "place"
where the meeting between God and man takes place. Even as
Church and Bible are signposts pointing beyond themselves to the
climactic events, so these very events point beyond themselves to

[4] W. Temple, *Christ's Revelation of God*, SCM, 1925, p. 8.

the encounter itself, to the meeting of God and man. Revelation, in other words, means "God" and not history.

Luther has said that God and faith belong together. The purpose of Christian preaching and worship is not exhausted on the level of asserting that the revelation is inextricably involved in the drama of salvation as recorded in the Bible. Where this has happened in the past reformers have recalled the Church from undue confidence in holy archaism to obedience to the Living God who "can of these stones raise up sons to Abraham." Revelation is completed only as individuals make responses of faith within the community and share in the lifelong task of appropriating the tradition. To appropriate tradition is no mere intellectual task; it means to be met again and again as a person in the depths of his knowledge, his moral allegiance, and his emotional loyalty by the Living God. It now becomes possible to develop the basic formula in the definition of revelation quoted earlier from Schmidt as "his giving of himself in communion."

This basic Biblical definition means a meeting between God and men. It means that the world of personal relationships offers us, by analogy, our knowledge of God. Here we are involved again in the interesting situation which we observed with reference to the meaningfulness of history. The reason our Western culture sets so high an evaluation upon the person is that the Biblical-Christian revelation in the person of Christ and the theological development behind the doctrine of the Trinity have become culturally assimilated. Most of our contemporaries who have abandoned the Christian faith still have a compulsion to establish the realm of the personal as the highest in experience. It might be argued that their attempt is reasonable only on the basis of distinctively Christian religious presuppositions, since most Eastern religions feel that a proper salvation would draw one away from the seductive illusion of personality to a non-personal principle of identity. Such a situation shows how much the de-

liverances of "common sense" and "reason" in any culture are products of a religious and philosophical tradition.

No book about personal relationships has found so widespread
an acceptance in current theological writing as Martin Buber's
I and Thou. It is an analysis of the twofold nature of the created
order—the world of things and the world of persons. Our age,
because of its great technological progress and its underlying
scientific orientation, is obsessed with the world of things. This
external world is often regarded as the only world about which
reliable knowledge can be secured. In many types of modern
philosophy knowledge has come to mean only those features of an
object that can be perceived by an observer. Materialism, whether
as an official metaphysic in communism or as the unavowed practical goal of multitudes in the West, testifies to modern man's obses-
sion with things. In the world of things I am at the center as master
and manipulator. Things are used by me as reacting "its." Even
people, when they are used as a means to the attainment of my
purposes, are degraded from their full stature as persons to the
level of objects.

The world of persons is for Buber the really significant world.
Here knowledge is not by observation but by participation and
communion with other selves. The basic sin of modern man is that
he treats persons as things, as so many reacting "its" rather than
as responsive "thous." "Real life is meeting." Like most prophets
with a strong message, Buber rather devaluates the world of
things, forgetting how communication between persons inevitably
involves things and that persons have a physical base in the world
of things. But what is of special interest in Buber's analysis is his
conviction that the knowledge of other persons comes not primarily by observation but as reception, as grace, as meeting. Unless
the other person will reveal himself to us we do not attain much
real knowledge about him. Man is not an isolated individual who
needs to learn how to relate himself to other peoples, as some
types of educational theory would suggest. Man, by his given na-

ture, exists in relationship to others. His spirit is not an attribute of his isolated self but a description of his indestructible relatedness to other selves.

"The Thou meets me. But I step into direct relation with it. Hence the relation means being chosen and choosing, suffering and action in one. The primary word I-Thou can be spoken only with the whole being . . . I become through my relation to the Thou; as I become I, I say Thou."

"Spirit is not in the I, but between I and Thou. It is not like the blood that circulates in you, but like the air in which you breathe. Man lives in the spirit, if he is able to respond to his Thou."[5]

It is significant that the singular pronoun of the second person has largely disappeared from modern English, betraying, perhaps, in grammatical usage the increasing objectification of persons from the primal "I-Thou" relationship to the derived "I-it" relationship. The survival of "Thou" in prayer testifies to the most personal of all relationships. According to Buber, the extensions of the lines from our personal relationships meet in the Eternal Thou.

Whether or not the Buber terminology is used, his analysis accurately describes the element without which revelation is not revelation but simply talk about revelation. God actually meets me. This is different from my discovering God as the ultimate principle of explanation or as the final value of existence. To use the vivid verbs of action which the Old Testament employs, God "comes" to me and "visits" me. In my appropriation of the dramatic saving events of the Bible I meet not a doctrine about God, not a special type of religious experience, although these are secondary products of the encounter, but I meet God himself. I meet him, moreover, in the person of Christ, which is perhaps only another way of saying that God so valued responsive personal relationships that he sent not a law, nor a prophet, nor a special rite, although all these are in the background, but he came himself. It

[5] Martin Buber, *I and Thou,* T. Clark, 1937, pp. 11, 39.

was in the fullness of a historic personality that God incarnated himself for man. "God was in Christ reconciling the world to himself."

The empirically unique element in Christianity among the religions of the world is the belief that a decisive and final revelation has happened in Christ and that the eternal Christ can become contemporary in revelatory experience for his followers. Those who speak about revelation generally mean a verbal transcript codified in law or expressed in the teaching of a final prophet. Locating revelation in the person of Christ has given Christianity a norm that is permanently revolutionary, for a person can never be exhaustively defined in words. He is richer than any event. Other religions have tended to become static as they attempted to safeguard the deposit of revelation in a new age with bewilderingly novel environmental situations. At times Christianity has succumbed to this temptation to conceptualize its revelation and to offer the doctrinal derivative as the real thing, whether in dogma or sacred text, but again and again the Holy Spirit has breathed new life into falsely deified tradition. It has then been experienced anew that God confronts man in living personal address.

What has become the center of revelation for Christians is thus both continuous and discontinuous with the revelation of the Old Testament. The provisional formula of event and believing interpretation is now telescoped into the person. Jesus of Nazareth is the event; and the believing interpretation of the event is expressed in the meanings given to the word Christ. The further development of this theme must await the next chapter, but the organic rootedness of this Christian revelation in all that has been previously developed remains to be indicated.

It is not Incarnation or Atonement as theological categories which indicate what a Christian means by his confession that in Jesus Christ he meets, or is met by, the Living God. Those theological categories are accurate and indispensable rationalizations or explanations, but they follow the reality rather than are identical with it. Even the phrase "revelation in the person of Christ" is a philosophical summary of something much more basic and dynamic. It is not God becoming man that saves, which, after all, is an idea, but this particular Christ, in all the particularity of his being, that is our Saviour. That is to say, it is the Christ of history who saves us. The theological notion that a Christ of faith could be substituted for the Christ of history was partly the rebound from a specially skeptical type of historical method and partly the subtle imperialism of theologians who wished conceptual tidiness for their systems at the expense of the scandal of historical particularity. To affirm that the Living God meets us in Christ is not to say that he lectures us on Incarnation and Atonement but that he presents a revelation of himself in a total life of sacrificial love and service. That life has its continuity with the life of prophets and of patriarchs. Here again the principle of continuity and discontinuity is at work.

Moses is called to his task in the experience of the burning bush. His message engenders opposition from the people who prefer the comfort of a golden calf to the Living God who smashes the idolatries of man. Isaiah's call results in suffering, in rejection, and, by tradition, in martyrdom. What is true of Moses and Isaiah is true in general of the experience of the men who speak God's Word in the Old Testament. Men are elected by God for a special mission; their fidelity to this mission creates opposition and persecution; they are faithful often unto death. The "Word" that comes to the prophet has verbal substance in that it points to the Holy and Righteous One of Israel, but the "Word" meets the prophet's contemporaries in their everyday responsibilities for social justice, international righteousness, and personal commitment. Faithful witness to that "Word" begets opposition. The clearest Old Testament apprehension that such is the fate of God's prophets is articulated in the poems of the Suffering Servant. Here the suffering and opposition are redemptively carried so that the nations perceive what has been done for them: "He was wounded for our transgressions. The chastisement of our peace was upon him." All of this dimly suggests that a perfect man, a perfect Suffering Servant, may be chosen in whom the "Word" revealed to prophets will become the enacted Word. It suggests further that such a one will inevitably arouse not men's praise and adoration but, and here is the tragic irony of the situation, their hostility and rejection. What God was communicating in the lives of the prophets, namely, a pattern of election, witness, suffering, and service, always disfigured by the sins of the prophets, will become perfectly transparent in a newly chosen One. In such a life, when it is appropriated in faith, man can be met by the Living God himself. God's "giving of himself in communion" will be translated into actuality when the Word is made flesh in the form of a Servant. The revelation that comes on the plane of history and the revelation that is perceived to be such only by the eyes of faith will be crystallized in a decisive manner in Jesus received as the Christ.

CHAPTER VII

Jesus Christ and Revelation

In an article in *The Interpreter's Bible* H. H. Farmer uses an interesting, although somewhat fanciful, illustration to show how God comes into human history in the person of Christ. He imagines one way by which a man might come "into" the history of a primitive people. He might be parachuted down into the tribe with power devices for compelling the tribe to accept the new type of life represented by the intruder. By fiat and the use of power he could presumably compel new sanitation practices, establish greater soil productivity, and mold their history to his image. But all of this would somehow remain external to the history or common life of the tribe. In the degree that the parachutist's invasion was successful their history would cease to exist and would be radically displaced by a new and unrelated history. Such a *deus ex machina* invasion is not the way of Christ. Another approach to the tribe might be to work "within" its history and common life, leading men by persuasion and example to a higher state of life in such a way that the newness of the invader's work remains organically related to the past. Their history has been changed but from within. This second method of approach roughly resembles the way of Christ. It would be action "in" and "through" the tribal history.

When God comes "into" history in the person of Christ he comes as a Jew within the structures of Judaism. The radical newness of the situation can be perceived only by eyes of faith, not by external evidence or compelling proof. Here we have the supreme example of the pattern of continuity and discontinuity which has served as a principle of interpretation for describing revelation.

It is the belief of Christians that Christ came in the fullness of time. The revelation which is looked upon as the supreme disclosure of God himself did not "just happen." It occurred when it did because God had been preparing a people to receive this revelation. The long and painful education of Israel under the Law and the prophets was the necessary presupposition for the encounter with God in Christ. Time is significant here, not so much in the quantitative sense of duration or clock time, but in the qualitative and existential sense of timeliness or "ripeness." Man, as a creature of space and time, discovers a new understanding of the time dimension of his existence when confronted by a revelation that presupposes a continuity with the "times" of Jewish history but is expressed in terms of a discontinuity of "fulfilled" time.

Not all have interpreted Christ's relation to history in this twofold manner. Within the Christian community and without there have been doctrines about the nature of Christ that have emphasized discontinuity at the expense of continuity. These are best illustrated by the school of theologians at Alexandria and by Marcion's radical rejection of the Old Testament Creator God for the redemptive God of Love exclusively revealed in Christ. There are theologians today who come very close to these positions. Others have emphasized continuity at the expense of discontinuity. The school of Antioch, in its Christologies, came near to this, as did the Ebionites, who saw in Jesus the true Messiah of Israel, but simply a man and no more. The so-called "solution" of the early controversies about the nature of Christ in the formula of the Council of Chalcedon attempted in the philosophical categories of that period to do justice to the perspective of both continuity and discontinuity. The "one person in two natures" terminology is troublesome in the changed philosophical vocabulary of our day, but it is a witness to the two basic convictions shared by every New Testament writer, although often quite differently expressed, that (1) Jesus is fully a man in every sense of the word and that (2) Jesus is somehow one with God himself.

It is just at this point that a great many people today call a halt. They will accept God, they say, and they will regard Jesus of Nazareth as the greatest religious teacher of men, but they refuse to bring these separate convictions together in the confession that Jesus is the Son of God. They see no necessary connection here and are bewildered by the doctrine of the Incarnation. They somehow feel that such a conjunction is not worthy of God and just a bit too presumptuous a claim to make for any man. The first critical question for those who take this position, and they are found inside the churches as well as outside, is: "What do you mean by God and what are the sources of your knowledge about him?" This question will be treated more fully in a later chapter. The next critical question is about Jesus as the greatest religious teacher: "Do we take the teaching seriously?" Sometimes the full facts of his teaching or, more important yet, their ultimate significance are not seriously examined.

The God of Jesus was the God of the prophets of Israel—One, Holy, Righteous, and Merciful. Jesus does not come to reveal a God not hitherto known at all but to reveal fully and in a final way a God already known in part to Israel. If Jesus is the great religious leader of men, it is strange that many who hold this position have not paid more attention to the piety of Jesus, to his teaching about God and his constant fellowship in prayer with him, for surely this is all part of the man. To be his follower, but to neglect the dimension of his living relationship to God, would be a strange contradiction. Many attempts have been made in the past to indicate the unique element in Jesus's teaching about God only to have this claim refuted by evidence from the Old Testament or from the rabbinic Judaism of his day. It has been said that Jesus was the first to call God "Father," but this paternal ascription can already be found in the Old Testament. He did, however, give to the father-son image of relationship a new development of intimacy—one that proved scandalous to the orthodox of his day. Sometimes it has been said that Jesus was the first to teach men that God loved them. This is refuted again by evidence from Hosea and other Old Testament writers.

There is, however, an element of uniqueness in this very area. It is the definition of just what God's love means. The word "love" carries no commonly accepted meaning; its special definition requires a revelation of meaning. Prior to Jesus's teaching, the love of God had been considered as the special favor of God to the pious and the righteous. God loved those who kept his Law and who loved him. What was really new in Jesus's teaching is that God's love is seen as indiscriminate as regards either the responsiveness or the lovableness of the object. God actually loves sinners and outcasts. This is the revolutionary element in Jesus's teaching about the love of God. The parables describe this radical out-searching and self-giving love. The shepherd does not wait for the lost sheep but leaves the ninety and nine to seek out the lost one. This love of God is perpetually reaching out in forgiveness. The parable of the prodigal son illustrates the father's readiness to be reconciled as it shows negatively the elder brother's lack of just this type of love. The love of God is not awarded to men on the basis of their merit but lavishly poured out by divine compassion. The laborers who have worked all day in the vineyard object to the same wage for workmen hired much later in the day. They are right to protest in the name of human justice, but this is precisely the point of the parable and the only point of comparison: God is gracious to men without respect to the hours of earned

merit. Montefiore, the Jewish scholar to whom Christians owe
much for his insights, has singled out this outsearching and self-
giving quality in Jesus's conception of God's love as the radically
new element that distinguishes his teaching from that of contemporary Judaism:

"The Rabbis attached no less value to repentance than Jesus
. . . They too welcomed the sinner in his repentance. But to *seek
out* the sinner and, instead of avoiding the bad companion, to
choose him as your friend in order to work his moral redemption,
this was, I fancy, something new in the religious history of Israel."[1]

If God does take the initiative and come to human need without requiring that man should first fulfill certain conditions of
righteousness and pious responsiveness—and this is the burden of
Jesus's teaching about God—then is it such a violent transition to
believe that he who gives such teaching about God is also the
human embodiment of just such a God? If God is accurately described by Jesus, and presumably those who accept Jesus as the
"greatest religious teacher of men" would agree, else they would
be in a strangely inconsistent attitude if they rejected the center
and heart of his teaching, then is not the Incarnation just the way
one would expect to find such teaching expressed? Jesus is the incarnate expression of the loving, outsearching God. It is just the
testimony of the life here that gives credibility to the teaching
that God's love is outsearching and spontaneous. The truth of the
teaching is confirmed by belief in the Incarnation.

Jesus loves outcasts, tax collectors (never a popular vocation,
but an especially corrupt one in his day), and all who fall short
of the social standards of righteousness. It is shocking to the moral
Pharisees that this man sits down to eat with such people. Part
of the hostility aroused by Jesus is due directly to his refusal to
confine his attention to the pious and good people. He speaks

[1] C. G. Montefiore, *Some Elements of the Religious Teaching of
Jesus,* Macmillan, 1910, p. 57.

ironically that he has come to save not the righteous but sinners. In the end he reveals the unlovableness of man when the responsible religious leaders of his day and the political authorities unite to destroy him. Such a ministry to outcasts threatens the very standards of religious morality as hitherto understood. At the end he who counseled Peter to forgive men seventy times seven took to himself the hostility of men and their unlovableness and said in his last moments of pain, when others would have denounced man's inhumanity and injustice: "Father, forgive them; for they know not what they do."[2]

The significance of Jesus's teaching about God is rescued from abstraction and theory by the belief that Jesus is himself the Incarnation of God's saving love. The Word spoken is really enacted in a historic life. A teaching about love or a law of love is expressed in the only ultimately meaningful way. It is embodied in a person. To say that Jesus is like the God whom he describes, and this was basically the approach of Arius and his followers, fails at the crucial point. The description of a God of such love as Jesus teaches needs the further corroboration of a life that expresses such a love *essentially*. A life that merely illustrated the teaching about such love would still fall under the suspicion of a poetic ideal. Only if Jesus is not merely like the God whom he describes, but is *essentially* that God, can faith grasp the full depth of the teaching. The teaching about God's indiscriminate love could only be established by an atonement which dealt with the moral demands of God in an act of God's self-giving. It would have to meet from one perspective the valid objections of the Pharisees that Jesus was subversive of morality. The teaching needed something more to make it both credible and authentic; it required a costly self-giving by God himself.

There are other elements than the definition of love in the teaching of Jesus that raise grave questions for those who would accept him as the "world's greatest religious teacher" but stop short of

[2] Luke 23:34.

the Christian confession that he is this because he stands in a unique relation to God. Jesus has a disturbing habit of placing himself where his contemporaries had been taught to place God. The cry of blasphemy raised against him was justified if this Nazarene carpenter had no further credentials. One of the earliest controversies recorded in Mark is that of the healing of the paralytic. When the orthodox among the onlookers are shocked that Jesus pronounces the forgiveness of sins he rubs salt into this wound by saying: " 'Which is easier, to say to the paralytic, "Your sins are forgiven," or to say, "Rise, take up your pallet and walk"? But that you may know that the Son of man has authority on earth to forgive sins'—he said to the paralytic—'I say to you, rise, take up your pallet and go home.' "[3]

This placing of himself at the point where his contemporaries had been taught to place God is given dramatic expression in his parable of the Last Judgment in Matthew. It is Christ who exercises the task of separating those who have done simple acts of service to their fellow men in his name from those who have not. Who is this man who exercises the judgment of God if he is not somehow one with God himself? He taught with authority, impressing his contemporaries by the manner and substance of his teaching as against the cautious casuistry of the scribes or those who, like the Sadducees, were safeguarding a past deposit of revelation. Authoritatively he sets aside the Mosaic Law on divorce in the name of higher principles. He breaks the strict Sabbath laws against activity by healing the needy and allowing his disciples to pluck grain for their use, saying that the Son of Man is Lord also of the Sabbath. A still more disconcerting feature is that, unlike the Christian saints whose biographies show that the more they approach holiness the more conscious they become of their sinfulness, Jesus never shows signs of personal penitence or confesses, as we and all men should have to confess, violations of the law of love. His relations with his Father are unclouded by personal

[3] Mark 2:9–11.

guilt and sin. It is just this feature that has enabled him to deal decisively with the sins of his fellow men.

From many points of view, then, an analysis of the actual content of Jesus's teaching leads us to ground beyond the humanistic appraisal of him as the "world's greatest religious teacher." If God is not in this man, then it may be paradoxically asserted that he is not such a good religious teacher, after all, but one dangerously close to megalomania and blasphemy. All of this has been reached without an analysis of the teaching he gave or that was attributed to him by the early community about his Messiahship or about other titles of interpretation. To the consideration of this difficult issue we must now turn.

The pattern of continuity and discontinuity is dramatically exhibited in Jesus's relation to the hopes of Israel. He comes as the Messiah, or the Elect One of God, in fulfillment of Jewish expectation, but his conception of the Messianic office is so radically contrary to the contemporary forms of Messianism that he is rejected by his own nation. The most primitive form of Messianic hope was the confidence that the sufferings of Israel among the nations would be ended by "the Day of the Lord," when Israel, by divine intervention, would be established as triumphant over her foes. This imperialistic expression of historical meaning is a common element in ancient cultures like the Egyptian, Babylonian, and Assyrian. It is a perennial temptation in all cultures, for nations, like individuals, are prone to reconstruct the world about themselves as the center and to identify the national struggle with the meaning of life itself.

Amos, it will be recalled, condemned this nationalistic version of hope in the interests of a universalism that began to redefine the dilemma of history not so much as a struggle between the nation and its enemies as a contest between an evil all too powerful in history and a good often unable to maintain itself. There was, however, no progressive displacement of the nationalistic horizon by the universalistic-moral one but a continued battle with such writings as Joel taking the former perspective and Jonah the latter, while many sections of Isaiah blend the two in unstable compromise. The good will be vindicated, but generally God will discover that the good is held by Israel or a reformed unit of the nation. The hope of a Davidic Messiah often meant a king endowed by special gifts of divine power to establish goodness with power over evil. In many variant forms the common element is a picture of a Messiah triumphant on the plane of history being received by faithful Israelites. When Israel was experiencing, in its painful Babylonian captivity, the suffering and humiliation of national defeat and the violence and injustice of its conquerors some were naturally tempted to dream of a military triumph and restoration of the nation or at least of a restoration that would vindicate the righteous remnant within Israel.

There were, however, profounder spirits who saw God revealing to them deeper insights about the suffering of the righteous and the sinfulness of all men. Their insights, never identified within the Old Testament itself with the Messianic hope as such, would cause a restatement of the problem of history on a much profounder level, for which the current forms of Messianism could offer no clear answer, but would prepare the way for Jesus's radical reinterpretation of Messianism. That rephrasing of the question would be along these lines: since even the relatively righteous are corrupted in their historic responsibilities by the misuse of power, are there resources of mercy in God beyond his needed judgment of all men that will solve this contradiction at the very heart of history? Or, phrased in shorter terms, can a Messiah without power answer the contradictions of historical power?

The Servant poems in the last half of the book of Isaiah express this new dimension of the problem. The Servant accepts his suffering, not stoically or combatively, but redemptively, as a sacrifice for sin, and the onlookers who witness the Servant's action respond by the recognition that, "He was wounded for our transgressions." As far as is known, the Servant figure before the time of

Christ was never identified with the Messiah but referred presumably to the nation or some ideal part of the nation. Jesus's use of the Servant figure in his teaching and its exemplification in his life were such radical departures from the popular dream of a powerful, triumphant Messiah that they became "stumbling blocks" to the Jews. They were not really grasped even by the disciples in their fullest dimensions until after the Resurrection. It will be recalled that Peter, after his confession at Caesarea Philippi that Jesus was the Christ, immediately rejected the subsequent saying of Jesus that the Son of Man, a figure from the apocalyptic book of Daniel, must suffer. Peter grasped only the old wine skin of Messiahship, not the new wine of a suffering Messiah. It would seem that one of the reasons for Jesus's reluctance to give direct teaching about his person was just the misunderstanding that a Messianic claim would inevitably stir up. When he was questioned about his Messiahship before the trial, as in his answer to the disciples of John the Baptist, he points to the works of healing and the message as indirect testimonies, adding, "Blessed is he who takes no offense at me."[4]

The question as to whether Jesus regarded himself as a suffering Messiah has been much debated among New Testament scholars. It would seem not unreasonable in the light of the actual evidence to conclude that the most probable reason that the community of the resurrection faith interpreted Jesus in these terms, and probably inserted details into the story of the life that brought out their conformance to prophecy, was the simple explanation that Jesus himself had interpreted his mission in these very terms. The saying that the "Son of Man also came not to be served but to serve, and to give his life as a ransom for many,"[5] much of the teaching of the last week of his life, such as the parable of the king and the wicked husbandmen, and the institution of the Last Supper as an enacted self-sacrifice converge to make this explana-

[4] Matthew 11:6.   [5] Mark 10:45.

tion more reasonable than the alternative one that all language about the Servant is simply due to the reading back into the historic record of the insights of the post-Resurrection community. This latter interpretation gives greater creativity to the group mind than history or psychology supports. Most coming events cast their shadows before. At the root of great and new developments in the history of religions is the impact of historical personalities.

Whatever may be the decision as to just how Jesus conceived his mission, there can be no doubt that every writer of the New Testament conceives him to be the Messiah or, if this phrase is not used, uniquely one with God himself. The earliest gospel, Mark, has as its first line: "The beginning of the gospel of Jesus Christ, the Son of God." Then follows a description by John the Baptist of the coming of a Messiah with a Baptism of the Holy Spirit, the special endowment of the Messianic Age. At Jesus's own baptism the writer reports a voice from heaven proclaiming, "Thou art my beloved Son; with thee I am well pleased."[6] Some scholars have seen in these lines from the second Psalm and from Isaiah the linking of Messiahship with the vocation of the Servant. Then follows shortly in Luke the preaching in the synagogue at Nazareth in which, after quoting from a Messianic passage in Isaiah, Jesus tells his fellow townsmen that "today this scripture has been fulfilled in your hearing."[7] It is obvious from the apostolic preaching as reconstructed from the book of Acts that one of its central affirmations was the Messiahship of Jesus declared by virtue of the Resurrection. Paul's description in Philippians of the condescension of Christ who, though "he was in the form of God," emptied himself, "taking the form of a servant," shows the same theme. It remained for the author of the Epistle to the Hebrews to relate the diverse strands of Old Testament revelation to the new and decisive center in Jesus Christ:

"In many and various ways God spoke of old to our fathers by

[6] Mark 1:11.   [7] Luke 4:21.

the prophets; but in these last days he has spoken to us by a Son,
whom he appointed the heir of all things, through whom also he
created the world. He reflects the glory of God and bears the very
stamp of his nature, upholding the universe by his word of power.
When he had made purification for sins, he sat down at the right
hand of the Majesty on high . . ."[8]

This passage indicates a transition from the Messianic-functional
titles to more inclusive ones of an incarnational nature. The two
types of categories are not be understood in radical antithesis but
as complementary. *Jesus is what he does and does what he is.*
One of the obvious reasons for the transition was the need to describe Christ in terms meaningful to Gentile Christians. Messiahship categories would not be immediately understandable to non-
Jews. Since the Jews were rejecting just this Messianic claim made
by the Christians for Jesus this whole approach was framed in confusion for a Gentile. The titles "Lord," "Son of God," and *Logos*,
or "Word of God," were more readily grasped because of associations in Gentile culture. The earliest of the Christian creeds,
"Jesus is Lord," is an ascription of immediate significance to a
Gentile because of analogy with owner-slave relationships or perhaps even by association with the "Lord" of a mystery cult, but it
is transformed by the specific use of the word "Lord" in the Greek
translation of the Old Testament for God himself. The filial-pater-
nal image has been the most meaningful for Christians in all ages
and cultures obviously because of the universality of the family
relationship itself. Its rootage in the teaching of Jesus gives added
support. His unique sense of dependence upon his Heavenly
Father, his special teaching that his disciples should in prayer address God as "Our Father," the scandal to the Jews of his famili-
arity with his Father as recorded in the Gospel of John—all point
to this title of interpretation as central. "All things have been
delivered to me by my Father; and no one knows the Son except

[8] Hebrews 1:1–3.

the Father, and no one knows the Father except the Son and any one to whom the Son chooses to reveal him."[9]

The title *Logos,* or "Word," as translated into English from the Gospel of John, is one of the most interesting. In its way it was as typical of Graeco-Roman culture as Messiahship was of Judaism. It received an altogether new significance by being transformed to describe the person of Christ. In the popular philosophy of the Graeco-Roman world it meant the ultimate principle of rationality upon which the universe was constructed. In the philosophy of the Alexandrian Jew, Philo, the *Logos* was somewhat assimilated to the creative function of the "Word" in the Old Testament. The Stoic background of the *Logos* concept, with its pantheistic over-tones, accounted for the principle of rationality being regarded as essentially divine. What was radically new when the writer of the Gospel of John chose this term for his Christology was the claim, quite unimaginable in terms of its past associations, that the *Logos* had become flesh in Jesus Christ. What had been a divinized principle became a historic person! These categories of more inclusive reference were necessitated by the missionary success of the early Christians. It was not an unmixed blessing, for the history of the Church shows too great a concentration upon some phrases to the neglect of those others that modify and qualify the few singled out in ecclesiastical controversy.

What is important to establish at this point is that all of the New Testament titles fail to exhaust the richness of the revelation in Christ. These titles are not the revelation in spite of a tendency in the history of the Church to offer some of them as though they were the revelation itself. The titles are verbal expressions only. They must not be eliminated or else all sinks into confusion, but they point beyond themselves to the fullness of Christ's life as the revelation. The titles witness to one element in the Old Testament revelation previously described. They indicate that God has chosen

[9] Matthew 11:27.

or elected this man in a decisive manner. It is to a mission so complete and so impossible that God alone can do it. Only if this chosen man is himself also God initiating the call can we understand the new dimension that fulfills and yet judges the Old Testament preparation in the vocation of patriarchs and prophets. Here for the first time the witness is completely one with the life, for the "Word has been made flesh." The message of Jesus and his healing works are indirect testimonies to the eyes of faith that a greater than the prophets is here. Just as the faithful witness of the prophets provoked persecution and suffering, so the utter faithfulness of Jesus to the will of God and his radical demonstration of sacrificial love begets rejection, persecution, and finally death. But God uses the wrath of man to praise him and transmutes the suffering and rejection of Calvary into new life and into a triumph over sin and death by the Resurrection. The last word was not God's judgment on man's erring judgment but an act of renewal, symbolized in the redemptive pattern of his activity in the Old Testament but now given decisive and final form and made available to those who respond in faith.

The next chapter must concern itself with the atoning act of Christ, especially as its appropriation in the community of faith throws more light on what is meant by a Christian's understanding of revelation as redemption. If God has fully revealed himself in Christ it remains also to consider how modern Christians can know this and be brought into relationship with these saving events.

CHAPTER VIII

Revelation and Redemption

One of the difficulties in the scholastic understanding of revelation is that it fails to show clearly that revelation in the Christian sense is also redemption. That is to say, the man who really knows God in terms of the Bible is by that very experience a man who is being reconciled to God. Knowledge of God means service of God. The scholastic division of the knowledge of God into a preliminary area accessible to human reason and an inner sanctum approachable only by faith in revealed dogma results, in spite of all attempts to the contrary, in intellectualizing revelation as though it were an extended branch of the knowledge of God accessible to reason. But this is seriously to misunderstand revelation. Revelation is not a type of knowledge comparable to scientific, mathematical, or philosophical knowledge. In these very important types of knowledge the self properly remains in the center as the collector of data, as the weigher of evidence, and as the file clerk for the memory of facts and evaluations. Such knowledge does not of itself transform or change the knower. It adds to his store of information, often making him increasingly skillful in changing his environment to fit his needs or wishes. Such knowledge may become the occasion for a transformation in character when study of the sciences strengthens the knower to respect truth wherever it may lead, even if it challenges the prejudices and special interests of the investigator. It is clear, however, when such a desirable result happens that it is not the accumulation of facts as such which changed the character. This knowledge was but the occasion; the change sprang from a shift in values held by the responsible self.

The knowledge of God as he is known from the Biblical revelation cannot be catalogued as an extension of this human quest for knowledge in spite of the obvious fact that language is the organ of communication of meaning in both types of knowledge. The knower of God cannot remain indifferent as a scientist might to the accumulation of details. Very little is added in terms of a store of verbal knowledge when man is met by God. Such knowledge, far from increasing the competence of the knower to change his environment, strikes at the very citadel of the sufficiency of the self. It actually transforms the self in the same way, although in a much more significant degree, that our close relationships to spouse and friends really mold our character. Revelation then is not the extension of our knowledge but *the painful transformation of our ideas and attitudes*.

It would be arrogant for a Christian to argue that disbelief in God was caused solely by the resistance of a willful self against God's moral demands, since there is such a thing as honest disbelief. On the other hand, it would seem that the unwillingness of the proud self to take God's moral demands seriously is much more widespread than generally admitted. Pascal says that it is so hard to believe because it is so hard to obey.

Another aspect of the redemptive character of revelation is that the man who has met God in Christ is immediately bound by that experience to his fellow men in new bonds of community. The Bible does not present the experience of revelation as the meeting of the Alone with the alone. The result of seeing Christ as the Son of the Living God is to see one's fellow men as those for whom Christ has died. There is a contrast here with the ordinary result of the scholar who sets out to amass technical knowledge. While there is such a thing as a companionship between scholars engaged in the same enterprise of discovery, yet the deeper the scholar penetrates beyond the commonly accepted results in his field the more likely he is to lose living contact first with the ordinary run of mankind and secondly with his fellow researchers. The specialist's very competence lessens his ability to communicate meaningfully from the frontiers of discovery. Ordinary knowledge can become a very isolating procedure, leaving the knower alone with his specialized objects of research. This isolating tendency is quite opposite to the knowledge of God which builds community and is furthered by increasing relations of witness to one's fellow men. Technical theology has often resulted in barriers to communication, but where this difficulty is present to an acute degree there must always be the suspicion that the theologian has lost his focus upon the "meeting" and, in his effort to describe this reality, has falsified it by overintellectualizing it and by subsuming it under just the type of scientific knowledge from which the experience is chiefly to be distinguished.

If it be true that revelation is misunderstood when it is regarded as an appropriate subject for filing in the contents of an encyclopedia of human knowledge, since it deals with the deeper experience of the meeting between selves rather than the amassing of subject matter, it now becomes important to ask what this means in terms of the Christ who is experienced as the heart of revelation. If revelation is correlated with redemption what is Christ's significance here?

We have used hitherto such expressions as Christ "the final revelation" or the "decisive meeting" between God and man. Are not these very claims contrary to the revelation itself? Do they not express pride and exclusiveness where Christ's life, as it has been maintained, expresses the Servant theme? By what right do those who claim to speak in the name of one who came not to be ministered unto, but to minister, use such language?

One of the deepest betrayals of the heart of the Christian faith has been a proud superiority on the part of some Christians to the other religions of the world. Often cultural details that have been purely accidental accompaniments of the Christian faith in Western culture have been absolutized. These accretions have at times been presented to men of other religions and cultures as possessing the sanctity of revelation itself. Such attitudes of institutional self-assertion and cultural naïvete are profoundly contrary to the spirit of the Christian revelation itself. But when confession has been made for these serious distortions does there not remain an irreducible citadel of pride in claiming finality for Jesus as the Son of God?

The answer to this question must be without hesitation or apology. Jesus Christ is the final revelation. The word "final" here can be readily misunderstood, however, if too much emphasis is placed upon its meaning as regards time rather than as regards purpose. In the sense that Jesus Christ was disclosed on the plane of history in years that can be measured chronologically the "final revelation" has happened. No Christian can regard this decisive event as simply the highest point in some history of revelation that may well be surpassed by some future revelation in history. Such an openness is from the Christian perspective false to the very way in which an individual comes to know Jesus as the revelation of God. It would reveal the detached attitude of a spectator who can never understand the reality of revelation because he fails to be a participant in it. When the Christian maintains that Christ is the final revelation of God he does not mean that the years 1–30 A.D. mark the "last" meeting between God and man. There is a continuous history of revelation in the Church, there is still a promise of Christ's return, but that continued "meeting" is not under new auspices but is based upon the center and criterion of all revelations in Jesus revealed as the Son of God.

The second meaning of "final" is more significant than its temporal sense. The revelation of Jesus as the Son of God expresses God's purpose for man. It sums up all other revelations by fulfilling them. The pattern of continuity and discontinuity is discernible in this understanding of Christ as the meaningful completion of all religions and all cultural quests for meaning. It now becomes possible to see that Christianity as a religion possesses no innate superiority to other religions. It, like them, is subject to judgment by the final criterion of all religions—Jesus as the Son of God. By what right then is the criterion asserted to be a final criterion?

The answer involves the heart of the Christian faith and illuminates the purpose of this chapter. Jesus reveals an unbroken unity with the God whom he addresses as "Father." His loyalty to this primary relationship involves him in conflict with his contemporaries. His method of dealing with this opposition is his continuous sacrifice of himself as the final revelation of God. That is to say, instead of establishing finite elements in his existence, such as special teaching, special customs or behavior, or special interpretations of himself as final expressions of revelation which would be idolatrous, he "loses" himself in the structures of life to the point where his Messianic being is subjected, contrary to popular notions of Messiahship, to suffering and extinction. Only that can be claimed as final revelation which sacrifices all its temporal, finite reality to God. Both the element of unbroken unity with the element of continuous servanthood are required.

The meaning of the temptations which are artistically presented by the writers of the gospels as "events" occurring at the beginning of his public ministry, but which were continuous experiences for him, present Jesus as struggling against the suggestions of the powers of darkness. They tempt him to elevate some element in his person or mission to unconditioned significance and to ground it by power in history where it need no longer be believed by eyes of faith but would be visible to all. Stones converted into bread, visible lordship over all kingdoms, a safe leap from the pinnacle of the temple—these would be convincing demonstrations of power, but they would also be idolatrous perversions of finite realities. The explicit protest of the disciples against Jesus's teaching that his Messiahship involved suffering and death and their despair when events confirmed the teaching testify to a hard core of resistance at just this point. Jesus's own struggle in the Garden of Gethsemane against the prospect of death expresses our human resistance to the surrender of "our power" and our inability to grant to evil the right of triumph on the plane of history over good. But the concluding affirmation, "Nevertheless, not my will but Thine be done," reveals that unbroken unity of purpose with God without which the self-sacrifice is merely martyrdom and not yet a final revelation of God.

The Christian claim that in Jesus there is not merely authoritative teaching about love as the fundamental principle in the universe but also an incarnation of God's love that can by this manner alone reveal its reality is given deeper meaning by the Christian doctrine of the Atonement. That is to say, a love which is defined in terms of selfless service of others and as making no claims for the self is revealed not merely by Jesus's teaching that God forgives but by a costly act of self-sacrifice by God in Christ, which is the only way it could be made real for men and translated from the realm of words and ideas into the sphere of deeds. Revelation is redemption.

Christian faith has always maintained the "necessity" of the Cross at the same time that it has realized the "scandal" of the Cross. On the surface it may seem strange to speak of the "necessity" of the Cross as expressing the will of God, for it is possible to describe the death of Jesus as the resultant of many human causes and wills—the hostility of the Jewish temple hierarchy and Pharisees, the actual betrayal by Judas of the disciples' retreat to the temple police, the political opportunism of the Roman governor, and the actions of soldiers carrying out orders to flog and crucify their prisoner. There is "scandal" enough here for contemporary Jewish Messianism and Graeco-Roman cultural urbanity almost to explain the "necessity" of the Cross, but all of these problems fade into the background when it is claimed that these events express the will of God. "For this reason the Father loves me, because I lay down my life, that I may take it again. No one takes it from me, but I lay it down of my own accord."[1]

This deeper necessity of the Cross is rooted in three realities: (1) the sinfulness of all men, (2) the moral order of the universe, not as an independent reality, but as established, sustained, and valued seriously by God, and (3) the overarching love of God. To appreciate that revelation is redemption requires us to understand the human situation in the light of the Christian faith.

The "trivialization" of the theological term "sin" in modern usage, in which it generally has come to mean some petty moral offense or some neurotic preoccupation with a guilt from which an enlightened psychotherapy would release man, is characteristic of an age which could not bear the affront to man's pride implied in its religious usage. Sin is properly a religious word denoting the breakdown in the relationship between God and man. Immorality and crime are primarily words describing a breakdown in relationships between men. They may also be considered as sin when they are understood in the vertical dimension as offenses against God's moral order. The most satisfactory definition of sin is "unbelief," not merely in the intellectual sense of a denial of theism, but as a total movement of man away from his intended relationship to God as the center of life. Such "unbelief" involves moral, practical, and emotional as well as theoretical elements. It is an existential situation in the sense that the whole man is actively and responsibly involved.

"Unbelief" may be further defined as "self-centeredness," provided that phrase is understood as an expression of the imperialism of the self rather than just a neutral description of finiteness. Man as an animal with a central nervous system and as a being

[1] John 10:17–18.

endowed by his Creator with self-consciousness will, under the conditions of our space-time existence, always remain a discrete organism that is geographically the center of its world. The self, in exercising the functions of vision, finds itself the center of observation about which the world of nature and other selves are grouped. The physical necessities of finitude which are not sinful readily become, however, a symbol for the activity of the self which wills to make itself the center of existence. The self will not accept its finiteness. The self wills to dominate the natural world; it wills to subject other selves to its whims; it wills to use God as a tool of the self's aggression, if it does not deliberately rule God out of the picture. The Christian faith has consistently maintained that this procedure is employed not simply by notoriously evil men but by us all. It has further maintained that, while the self is responsible for this development, it is beyond the power of the self, in spite of the best resolutions to the contrary, to extricate itself from this impasse. There is a paradox in sin that man is responsible and yet sin is inevitable. The movement of the self out of the divinely purposed system of mutual relationships of love between men leads to corporate expressions of sin in which the self relates itself to imperialistic strategies on the part of family, class, race, or nation. Men will do for their limited group what they would not do for themselves. Here again it is not within the power of the self by thought or unaided action to extricate itself from the tangled web of human sinfulness and guilt.

St. Paul has clearly stated what might be called the paradox of moralism on the analogy of the paradox of hedonism. Many philosophers have seen that the deliberate attempt to achieve happiness by calculated strategies of pleasure is usually self-defeating. Happiness comes as a by-product when the self is serving other goals. Likewise the deliberate and self-conscious attempt to raise the self to higher obedience to the moral demands of the universe, although the self is capable of definite improvement, never fulfills its aim. The outstanding limitation of an ethic founded simply upon itself and without religious rootage is that it cannot attain its highest goals. St. Paul confesses that the good which he wanted to do he did not do and the evil which he wanted to avoid he actually did. Here the Biblical analysis of the human predicament has greater depth of realism than the characteristic analysis made in Greek culture. Aristotle holds that if a man knows the good he will do it. Evil action springs from ignorance. In the Christian frame of reference we confess that we are unable to achieve the perfection which we feel impelled to attempt to realize and we dare not excuse our guilty shortcomings by asserting our ignorance. Where ignorance is a strong factor it often is willful ignorance.

One of the commonest forms of sin is pride. Pride of power is tragically illustrated in the competing nationalisms which are driving our world toward destruction. Individual pride is compounded in group pride. Pride of knowledge, pride of goodness, and religious pride are sublimations of that basic motivation in man which drives him to assert his own lordship in the world rather than to accept and obey the true Lord of life. The attempt to reduce or eliminate the ravages of pride is an obvious imperative in our day. For purposes of analysis, let us examine the honest moralist who is sincerely desirous of conquering pride in his own life. He resolves at the start of the day to show less pride in all his associations with people. At the end of the day he reviews his real progress. He actually was less proud in his bearing with the people he met. Only now, in even more sensitive honesty, he realizes that he is proud of the day's accomplishment. Tomorrow he must fight harder: he must increase in humility and not take pride in his achievement. When he is rigorously honest with himself he realizes he is caught in a recessive situation from which he cannot extricate himself. His substantial progress is threatened by valetudinarian anxiety about the irrepressibly proud self. He is like a man caught in a swamp whose strenuous efforts to free himself result only in his becoming more deeply mired. When he evaluates the situation responsibly he discovers that he cannot himself remove his guilt without destroying the very foundations of morality.

If we further complicate the situation by adding group pride the plight of the honest moralist becomes even more insufferable. How can an American citizen atone for the pride of his nation in its relations with its own allies, not to speak of its even more difficult relations with its political and economic enemies? No matter how humble the individual American may be he cannot, as a citizen, absolve himself from responsibility for the proud and over-bearing actions of his government on the less powerful nations of the world. How does a white American who may personally have almost no racial prejudice atone for the characteristic injustices of a majority racial group? One of the many morally perplexing problems of the pacifist in America is that his refusal to bear arms does not absolve him from the guilt of paying taxes to a government that keeps itself alive in history by military preparedness. Even if he refuses to pay taxes the peaceful security of the prison in which he may be placed is upheld by American power. In none of these group situations can we extricate ourselves completely from responsibility or guilt.

The moral life pursued in honesty and without self-deception leads not to victory but despair. The Christian analysis would be a most depressing one if it led only to this. Fortunately it does not. The Christian Gospel proclaims that God met this moral impasse by himself carrying the guilt and sinfulness of men in an act of infinitely costly self-sacrifice at Calvary. Because the moral demands in the universe are the expression of God's holy demands of righteousness only God could deal with this situation. Yet since it was man and not God who had created this situation only a man could be the responsible agent to accomplish God's purpose. Here is the "necessity" of the God-man who makes atonement for human sin. Yet if God simply declared a free forgiveness on the basis of human repentance this would violate the very moral foundations of the world. God's love would be revealed as an amoral, if not an

immoral, reality. The Cross, an act of divine suffering and humiliation, guards God's righteousness while he forgives. Divine forgiveness springs out of this great reconciling act in which Christ died
for the sins of the whole world—not merely for especially responsive people but for all men in all times and places.

It might be asked whether man cannot of himself effect reconciliation with his fellows. Cannot man ask forgiveness for his own
bad actions of those whom he has wronged? Cannot he be ready
to forgive others? While both courses of action are necessary as
parts of the total atoning act of God they must be seen as imperfect human expressions of a perfect atoning act by God instead of
substitutes for it. It is simply beyond a man's power to recall the
evil consequences of his actions. They have spread beyond his
knowledge, infecting ever widening circles. Our own repentance,
moreover, is never a pure act. Our desire for reconciliation, partly
based upon genuine shame and contrition, may also partly be based
on notions that we must get ourselves out of isolation into a restoration of relationships. Forgiveness is then exploited as a method.
Much "patching up" between husband and wife falls short of perfect reconciliation because of the interested motives of the participants. Far from being a substitute for a needed act of perfect
reconciliation, which only God could make, human activities of
reconciliation are understood by the Christian as springing from
the power of the Cross.

We are now at the very center of a Christian's knowledge of
God. He knows, or more properly is known by, the God who has
redeemed him and all mankind in the Cross. His recognition of
God's reconciling love, while it is stated propositionally and requires intellectual comprehension, is primarily a reality that involves him as a person. It means that he must allow himself to
be changed by opening his whole life to God. This knowledge of
God is a transforming, community-creating knowledge. The man
may be expected to win battles over pride now because he is
freed of excessive concern with the self and preoccupation with

its problems. The new life in Christ spontaneously brings new powers that, almost as by-products, help to transform the man from the old proud self into the image of the Christ of humble service. The most dreadful corruption of Christianity, however, comes when the very religion that strikes a death blow at human pride becomes a vehicle of religious pride in itself. Unfortunately for the Gospel and for history, Christianity has produced at times Christian Pharisees much more dangerous than their Jewish counterparts against whom so much of Jesus's teaching was directed.

Another way of expressing the truth that revelation is redemption is in terms of a definition of love. The word love has no commonly agreed upon definition. In Greek culture the word *eros* was generally employed to express sexual love based upon attraction between the sexes. Springing from a desire to be united with the object of love, *eros* was capable of sublimation along many lines. Shared interests might replace sexual attraction to produce "Platonic love" between the sexes or friendship between members of the same sex. The basic drive here is self-fulfillment based upon attraction. The object of love calls forth a response in the lover.

There is another meaning to love which usually modifies the situation previously outlined. The new kind of love is a selfless concern for the good of the loved one. Man and wife find romantic love deepened into forgiving love, in which a reciprocity between giving and receiving is established. Parents sacrifice themselves quite unselfishly at times for their children. Friends can reflect in their mutual relationships a costly redeeming love. "Greater love has no man than this, that a man lay down his life for his friends."[2]

The New Testament describes this second type of love as *agape* in order to distinguish it from *eros*. As a word, it is not particularly prominent in the teaching of Jesus, notwithstanding Jesus's definite teaching about the Great Commandment and about its sphere of operation in such a parable as the Good Samaritan. The word

[2] John 15:13.

becomes a key word for St. Paul and the writer of the Gospel of John. What made this word a central affirmation of Christian faith was not its centrality in Jesus's teaching so much as its dramatic realization in the life and death of Jesus. God defines love not by a verbal definition in a sacred dictionary but by loving men in Christ all the way to the Cross:

"While we were yet helpless, at the right time Christ died for the ungodly. Why, one will hardly die for a righteous man—though perhaps for a good man one will dare even to die. But God shows his love for us in that while we were yet sinners Christ died for us."[3]

St. Paul's magnificent definition of love in the thirteenth chapter of I Corinthians was the result of reflection upon the person who incarnates the atoning love of God. Expressed now in propositional speech, it can become again and again for the Christian a signpost leading him to "meeting" with Jesus Christ.

The revelation of this divine love builds a community of response. The Church is created to be a redemptive fellowship of love serving all mankind. He who knows that God is love is by that experience of revelation being transformed into the image of the Servant and being drawn into a shared life with his fellow men. Revelation is not propositional statements about a supreme being called God. Revelation is "meeting" the God who "was in Christ reconciling the world to himself, not counting their trespasses against them, and entrusting to us the message of reconciliation."[4]

Such revelation is redemption.

[3] Romans 5:6–8.   [4] 2 Corinthians 5:19.

CHAPTER IX

Revelation and the New Testament Church

In the two preceding chapters considerable emphasis has been placed upon the objectivity of certain great acts of God in history. After a preparatory communication to Israel God "came" in the person of Jesus Christ as the final or purposive revelation. He revealed in Christ that self-sacrificing love is at the heart of reality. The Christian knows God then through the Incarnation and the Atonement. Unless, however, men actually see God in these events, events that are quite capable, from a purely historical point of view, of being described as the clash of a Galilean prophet with the entrenched religious and political forces of his nation's capitol, no meaningful revelation would actually have taken place. The event requires a believing interpretation.

It might be argued that even if no one had recognized Jesus as the Christ or as dying for the sins of the whole world the Incarnation had still occurred. A waterfall in Siberia never yet seen by man presumably creates a thunderous roar, but, on the other hand, since no man has heard it can it be described as making a noise? The Biblical understanding of revelation is that the event cannot be separated from the believing interpretation of it. Men had to respond to and recognize the great saving events of God before the revelation had essential meaning. In this sense the believing response of the early community is part of the series of revelatory events and shares in the revelation itself. The witness of the apostles and their experiences became and can become for succeeding generations of Christians occasions for "meeting" the God who was and is in Christ.

Thus the Church has an organic and not merely an accidental relationship to the events of Christ's life, death, and Resurrection. Any attempt to establish a "churchless" type of Christian faith is a self-contradiction. There exists a widespread movement among intellectuals in Japan today to accept Christ as the revelation of God but to remain disassociated from any forms of Church life. Partly this position is a judgment on the brokenness of the contemporary Christian community and a reaction against the divisiveness of some types of missionary activity. But chiefly it exhibits the survival of a strong pagan individualism in Japanese culture paralleled, of course, by an indigenous individualism in our own Western culture. From both of these perspectives the Church appears as expendable.

Why not Christ as God's self-revelation without the Church? Does not Christ stand out all the more strongly without the embarrassment of the historic churches with their pettiness and compromises? The answer to these and similar questions is that the Church is an organic part of the Gospel. The knowledge of Christ has been mediated to these sensitive individuals by a historical community of faith. This fact, however, might still be regarded as accidental. Even the statement of this new gospel of "Christ alone for the individual without the Church" tends to build up a loose association between those who hold this belief as opposed to members of the historic churches, but the situation might still be assessed as an accidental element springing from natural human gregariousness. All such individualistic points of view fail to understand the Biblical meaning of revelation and the ways by which the revelation in Christ actually came and comes into history. The Old Testament writers understand that God saves men not as isolated individuals, each with an exclusively vertical relationship to God, but as men set also in a context of horizontal relationships with their fellow men in such manner that if the whole man is to be redeemed his community must also be redeemed. Personal and social salvation are not opposite but complementary aspects. This is the belief behind the concept of "the people of God." It is true that out of a primitive tribal collectivism in Israel the individual emerges later as a responsible subject of direct religious experience, as illustrated in Jeremiah and Ezekiel, but this increase in maturity in stating the relations between man, fellow men, and God is never an expression of sheer individualism with a negative evaluation of the claims of the community. Jesus, when betrayed and deserted by his friends and delivered into the hands of the hostile religious and political leaders of his society, becomes in his solitary person the whole people of God. Arbitrarily to stop the development there and to claim thereby some justification for a Christian individualism fails to perceive the organic relationship of the apostles' faith to God's saving acts themselves.

It is not merely that the apostles happened to be the first to understand the inner significance of the manger and the Cross in the sense that we can now dismiss them as a mere educational aid in achieving our own individualistic point of view. The truth is that we can never dispense with the apostles and the prophets, for they are not merely the historical steppingstones but the indispensable guides through whom and in the company of whose true followers it is only possible for us to meet anew the God who was in Christ. The Church is a continuous part of God's plan for dealing with men. He wills to incorporate believing individuals into it, for the Church is defined in the New Testament not as an institution with a vertebrate structure but as God's dwelling place with men. "You are fellow citizens with the saints and members of the household of God, built upon the foundation of the apostles and prophets, Christ Jesus himself being the chief cornerstone, in whom the whole structure is joined together and grows into a holy temple in the Lord; in whom you also are built into it for a dwelling place of God in the Spirit."[1]

The situation of the apostle as a mediator of the final revelation and his significance as the turning point in the subsequent history of revelation in the Church as based upon his response can be illustrated in terms of the Buber terminology of "I-Thou" and "I-it" previously discussed. When at Caesarea Philippi Peter confesses, "Thou art the Christ," he is caught up in the experience of "meeting" and makes a response on the fullest personal level to God. This revelatory moment belongs to the "I-Thou" type of human experience. "Thou art the Christ." This is a primary experience. Without this recognition and similar apostolic testimony there is no real revelation of God in Christ. When Peter, after the Resurrection, preaches boldly to the Jews that Jesus is the Christ, or the Messiah, he has turned half circle and now addresses the world with a message expressed in the third person "he" and no longer in terms of "thou." This belongs to the "I-it" type of experience, for in turning from the encounter itself to describe the person met, in order that others may share the experience, it is necessary to describe the meeting in objective terms. This is a secondary or derivative experience.

Another way of stating this twofold function typified by Peter is to describe the difference between worship and witness. The worshipping Church concentrates upon making possible renewed experiences of meeting God for those already within it. The missionary Church preaches its message to the whole world that more people may be drawn within its fellowship of response. Historically these two facets of Church life have not always been maintained in dynamic interrelationship as they were in the early Church. The Church has periodically been tempted to center its life about

[1] Ephesians 2:19–22.

itself and to regard its mission as one of bringing strength to those already within its doors. In this way worship becomes corrupted and introverted. To keep it wholesome worship requires witness and activity. The New Testament actually speaks much more about the necessity for witness and evangelism than it does about worship.

If any one of the events in Christ's life is to be singled out as chiefly responsible for the establishing of the Christian Church it must be the Resurrection. At the Crucifixion the disciples had fled; one had betrayed Jesus, and another had denied him. At the moment of his death Jesus represents in his own person the whole people of God. Only he remains obedient to God's will. As the physical body disintegrates under torture it is to be replaced by the mystical body of those who acknowledge him as Lord. The point of transition from the body of flesh to the Church as the body of Christ is the Resurrection. Often this event is wrongly evaluated in contemporary interpretation. The Resurrection is presented as the great miracle which alone is responsible for the existence of the Church. What is forgotten in this oversimplified reading of the event is that those who believed that he had risen from the dead and who saw him in his Resurrection appearances saw him not simply with the eyes of flesh, in unimpeachable proof, but primarily with the eyes of faith. The risen Messiah was not so objectively manifest to Roman officials and to the Jews in general that they immediately accepted him as Lord. Such a miracle of sight would have destroyed the inner requirement of faith which characterized his whole earthy mission. It would be inconsistent with the way God dealt with men in the whole Biblical record. In other words, the Resurrection appearances must not be falsely isolated from the believing response of the disciples. Nothing is more certain in the message of the early community than that Christ has risen from the dead. "If Christ has not been rasied, then our preaching is in vain and your faith is in vain."[2] This note is continuously repeated;

[2] 1 Corinthians 15:14.

it becomes a basis for appeal in the ethics and in the understanding of history in the Christian movement.

In the Cross Jesus won his victory over sin and the forces of darkness, but that victory remained hidden from men until they were enlightened by the Resurrection. Western Christian tradition, in both its Catholic and Protestant versions, has failed to make the Easter event as central to the living faith of its people as did the early Church or as the Eastern Churches have done in their liturgy and ecclesiastical calendar. Here is an area in which the Western tradition can be enriched as it learns through the Ecumenical Movement more about the Orthodox Churches and their life. Easter was necessary for the disciples. The outsearching love of God which they had experienced during their companionship with the earthly Jesus they now saw was no chance happening. He in whom they had seen the marks of Messiahship, only to be scandalized when the story ended with a criminal's death, had risen from seeming failure and defeat. Not only had he conquered *sin* but also *death* as well. Although they had fled from the scene of his last days in panic and in disappointment he had returned to them. He would not abandon them in their weakness. The love which he had taught them in his parables, as seeking out the lost sheep by leaving the ninety and nine, had actually sought them out again in spite of their disloyalty and cowardice. Now they knew that nothing could defeat this complete outpouring of the divine love. This love was not merely heroic; it was and would be victorious, for it was written into the heart of the universe. It was no longer an ideal but the *real*.

It was a revaluation of the meaning of Christ's life from the new perspective of faith in his Resurrection that caused them to understand the true significance of the revelation under the old Covenant. He was truly the Messiah in spite of his shameful death. He was the Messiah by virtue of this very suffering and by his Resurrection, which represented to the eyes of faith God's seal of approval upon his mission of servanthood. Here continuity and discontinuity become transparent to faith. These themes are movingly developed in the Emmaus appearance recorded in the Gospel of Luke.[3]

The incident deserves quotation here as an illustration of the faith response as an ineradicable element in the Resurrection appearances. This is especially necessary since too little attention has been given to it, due to a developing apologetic interest, even in the early community, to stress the objectivity of the event at the expense of the believing interpretation of the event.

"That very day two of them were going to a village named Emmaus, about seven miles from Jerusalem, and talking with each other about all these things that had happened. While they were talking and discussing together, Jesus himself drew near and went with them. But their eyes were kept from recognizing him. And he said to them, 'What is this conversation which you are holding with each other as you walk?' And they stood still, looking sad. Then one of them, named Cleopas, answered him, 'Are you the only visitor to Jerusalem who does not know the things that have happened there in these days?' And he said to them, 'What things?' And they said to him, 'Concerning Jesus of Nazareth, who was a prophet mighty in deed and word before God and all the people, and how our chief priests and rulers delivered him up to be condemned to death, and crucified him. But we had hoped that he was the one to redeem Israel. Yes, and besides all this, it is now the third day since this happened. Moreover, some women of our company amazed us. They were at the tomb early in the morning and did not find his body; and they came back saying that they had even seen a vision of angels, who said that he was alive. Some of those who were with us went to the tomb, and found it just as the women had said; but him they did not see.' And he said to them, 'O foolish men, and slow of heart to believe all that the prophets have spoken! Was it not necessary that the Christ should suffer these things and enter into his glory?' And beginning with

[3] Luke 24: 13–35.

Moses and all the prophets, he interpreted to them in all the scriptures the things concerning himself."

The disciples had to understand that a Messiah so discontinuous with popular expectation as to be rejected just because of his death at the hands of men was really continuous with the deepest insights of the previous revelation to Judaism. He was the Messiah precisely because of his suffering. The vocation of the Suffering Servant set forth in the writing of the second Isaiah was now seen to be the essential content of the Messianic hope rather than the Jewish misconception and corruptions of that hope. This Emmaus episode tells exactly how the disciples recognized their walking companion as the risen Christ. The simple, everyday nature of the event, so utterly like the simplicity of him whom they had known during his ministry as their table companion, is filled with significance for future generations of Christians who would know Christ in the celebration of the Lord's Supper. Here is a point of transition from the everyday companionship at meals and the solemnization of this fellowship on the night before his death to the Church as the mystical body of Christ. The Church is constituted in the confessions of many churches by the preaching of the Word of God and by the celebration of the Gospel sacraments. The simple naturalness of the event at Emmaus suggests at once the need for keeping the future ecclesiastical responses always in close association with these simple acts of table fellowship, lest they develop into specialized religious institutions, no longer pointing to their origins, but becoming sacred mechanisms with a false independence of their own.

"When he was at table with them, he took the bread and blessed, and broke it, and gave it to them. And their eyes were opened and they recognized him; and he vanished out of their sight. Then they told what had happened on the road, and how he was known to them in the breaking of bread."

Those who seek for the knowledge of God primarily in the field of the mathematical analysis of the universe or as the idea of the absolute in philosophy will find the preceding narrative naïve, if not shockingly anthropomorphic. Yet it expresses just that knowledge of God which is central for the Christian faith, for its primary field of concern is neither mathematics nor philosophy but the understanding of what constitutes a person in his relationships with his fellows in a historical setting. That the Creator of the universe should disclose his Son to some tired travelers in the breaking of bread may confound those "who seek after wisdom," but when the episode is seen by the eyes of faith it reveals "Christ the power and wisdom of God."

The Resurrection appearances cease after a time as though God himself wills to found the faith of the community less upon a repeated series of encounters with the risen Christ than upon a deepened understanding of *all* the events centering around his life reflected through a chain of human witness. Such is the task of the Church to point to Christ. Such is the significance of the Bible as the criterion of the Church's witness. Jesus left behind no book composed by him; he left behind no commandments written upon stone. He left instead *a company of people* charged to bear witness to him. Here was "the deposit" of the revelation as he left it.

The account of the Ascension in Acts is probably best described as the last of the Resurrection appearances to the community. The conviction that Christ would soon return is deeply rooted in the early documents of the New Testament. By all evidence it was an essential element in the early preaching, influencing, for example, St. Paul's attitude to slavery. Since the time for His return was near there was not much expectation of having to face the redemption of such social structures as slavery by the imperative of the love shown in Christ. In the letter to Philemon St. Paul deals solely with the personal relationship between Onesimus, the runaway slave, and his master and not with slavery as a social institution. The eschatological message of the early Church that the end times are approaching with the imminent return of

Christ has grated harshly on modern ears partly because the early disciples were plainly mistaken in their nearsighted dating of the event. Partly the fantastic speculations of various sects and movements in Christian history, claiming knowledge of the exact date of the end, have discredited by perversion and caricature the early hope of the community. Partly modern man, until quite recently, has had such unbounded confidence in his ability to mold history to his desires that he saw no need for such a redemption of history. It would from this perspective be a meaningless embarrassment. The seriousness of our times together with the discrediting of hope in man's complete mastery over history has brought new relevance to the eschatological hope of the early community. It has been translated in our day into a philosophy of history. The major theme of the World Council of Churches at the Evanston Assembly was the restatement for today of "Christ the Hope of the World."

The hope that Christ will return again is the expression of a confidence that history will not ultimately defy its own norm. We now see the sacrificial love shown in the Cross as struggling to maintain itself in our history. By faith, and at times by sight, we find it victorious when friends are reconciled after serious differences and when husband and wife, strengthened by the Cross, find renewal in the tensions of married life. Furthermore, there are signs that forgiveness based upon this type of self-giving love wins its victories in the more complex associations between groups of people. There is often a recognition on the part of labor and management that something more than a just contract is needed if the two sides are really to work together and not become fenced-off rivals, debating the wording of a contract and accusing the other side of aggression or violation. That something more than justice is dimly apprehended as a "spirit of give and take," which is a very rough approximation to the love revealed in the Cross. When two nations like France and Germany have been pitched against each other in a series of wars no ultimate resolution of their hostility is possible short of forgiveness. It is even less permissible here than in the example of labor-management relations to hope that justice will provide a means of reconciliation. Few industrial contracts are expressions of pure justice; they usually modify the special dictation of the more powerful of the group forces, with some considerations of fair play as understood in the general community in which the special tension has arisen. But nations victorious in warfare are notoriously blind to the imperatives of justice, as nearly every peace treaty shows. There is, moreover, no supranational community politically competent to enforce canons of fair play. If justice is difficult here, forgiveness is more so, although the need for it is clear.

While it is true that the Cross wins victories now on the plane of history as we know it, it is just as true that these victories are continually being frustrated by human sinfulness. There is no guarantee that the love revealed by Christ will maintain itself over the disruptive forces of evil in our history. Progressive subjection of history to the norm of this love may be hoped for, but there is no assurance in the New Testament that it will be accomplished by itself. Here is the inner significance of the hope in Christ's return. History itself requires redemption. Just as the Resurrection of Christ meant to the disciples who could see its significance that Christ had won his victory over death "to become the first fruits of them that slept," so the Christian who awaits the return of his Lord in glory expresses the confidence that history itself will be redeemed from its powerful evils and frustrations. Our concern is not with the fanciful imagery of trumpets and clouds which are, after all, only symbolic descriptions of an end of our space-time manifold. It can only be described symbolically because it is of an order past our experience. If it is described it must be described as an event in history which is self-contradictory, since its essence is that it transcends history.

One of the symbols pointing to the redemption of history is the creedal phrase "the resurrection of the body." It has been subject to serious misunderstanding. On the one hand, it was devaluated

by those who preferred the Greek concept of the immortality of
the soul as being somehow more "spiritual" than the Hebraic expression. In origin the Greek phrase was a rationalization on the
plane of philosophy of the primitive animistic belief in the survival
of soul-substance. In most of its Greek associations there was no
thought of the survival of personality. That the phrase is so used
by many today is the result of its having taken on the richness of
the Christian belief that could more adequately be expressed by its
indigenous symbol of the resurrection of the body. Such a symbol
does justice to man in the fullness of his existence as a creature of
body and spirit. It implies no depreciation of the body as such. It
symbolizes the historical quality of human existence by relating
the resurrection of the individual to the general resurrection at the
Second Coming of Christ. It has sometimes been wrongly ma-
terialized to mean the resuscitation of a grave body, in defiance of
St. Paul's warning that "flesh and blood cannot inherit the Kingdom
of God" and that what is sown is a "natural body" but what is
raised, not by its inherent immortality, but by the grace and power
of God, is a "spiritual body." Here again the continuity is modified by discontinuity. The fact that our history is not simply a
meaningless interlude, destined to be canceled out, is expressed
in the word "body" and in the identity of the coming Christ with
the Christ who came once into history. The fact that history cannot complete itself or redeem itself, and that if left to itself would
surely die, is represented by "resurrection" instead of "immortality" and by the return in glory of the Lord who came first as the
Servant.

The eschatological understanding of the early community of
faith had and has its significance for the Christian knowledge of
God. It was recognized that everything had not been made completely transparent by the revelation of God in Christ. There were
still some acts to be played in the drama, and we were still view-
ing the events before the final curtain. A Shakesperean tragedy
looks different when it is viewed as a finished drama than when

seen from some act before the last. In spite of the Christian conviction that God had fully revealed himself in Christ it was not maintained that no problems remained. It was not only a revelation that could be seen only by the eyes of faith; it could, even with the eyes of faith, be seen only in part.

". . . as for knowledge, it will pass away. For our knowledge is imperfect and our prophecy is imperfect; but when the perfect comes, the imperfect will pass away . . . For now we see in a mirror dimly, but then face to face. Now I know in part; then I shall understand fully, even as I have been fully understood."[4]

This warning has not always been heeded by the Christian Church. Far too often it has been assumed that because Christ was the final revelation of God it would follow, of necessity, that our statements about that final revelation would possess finality themselves. Men of faith found it difficult to understand that they had this treasure in earthen vessels. The God who has revealed himself in Christ has not given a partial revelation of himself but a unique and final self-disclosure of his very being. This did not mean, however, that Christian dogma was a final revelation. On the contrary, dogma was a partial, human description subject to the thought forms of the day and needed restatement in every succeeding generation. Surely there is nothing strange here. When we attempt to describe the influence of a great friend upon us we are aware of how imperfectly we can reduce the reality of the person to a few written paragraphs. The feebleness of our biographical statements, however, does not make us skeptical that we have ever known or met the friend. If, moreover, we anticipate that our friend will be even more helpful to us because we are about to work together on a project we should feel even more inadequate about our biographical sketch. We should not want it to be regarded as a final description of that person, but we should look forward to revising it as we came to know the friend more intimately in the future. It would be quite fantastic to focus atten-

4 1 Corinthians 13:8–12.

tion on the written transcript rather than on the person described therein. Likewise the early Church of the New Testament period shows little interest in officially defining dogma. Its eyes are still upon the God who reveals himself in Christ and who will more fully reveal himself, it is believed, in the Second Coming of Christ.

The events of Resurrection and Ascension are understood as points of transition in weaning the faith of the community away from the physical, bodily presence of Jesus. Otherwise the disciples and the apostles who associated with him in the days of his flesh remain privileged persons to whom later generations of Christians can only turn envious eyes and sing somewhat nostalgically: "We should like to have been with him then." But even as Christ sacrificed himself as the final revelation so that no finite element in his life could be grasped as "the revelation," so now in response to this transfiguration of Christ through his death and Resurrection there must correspond a change in the quality of the believing interpretation by the community. The Christ who was bound in his earthly life to the body of a Jew living in Palestine within a definite span of years must become available, apart from the limitations of space and time, to men of faith in all places and in all times. That is the inner significance of the Ascension of Christ to sit, in the creedal phrase, "on the right hand of the Father from whence he will come to be our judge." What is stressed here is not disappearance into the distance but universal availability. The particularism of the final revelation passes into a universalism. The Jewish Messiah is revealed as the Son of God not exclusively to the old chosen people, who were bound to a national culture, but now to a new chosen people who are to be called from all nations. The point of transition in the deepening of this believing interpretation of the community is the event of Pentecost. In origin Pentecost celebrated the wheat harvest and, by that alchemy in the Old Testament revelation that transmutes a festival of nature into a commemoration of history, it had come to mean by Christ's time a thanksgiving for the revealing of the Jewish Law as the

foundation event for the Jewish Church. A still deeper conversion
from the Law to the Spirit would take place in the new Pentecost.

The book of Acts presents a colorful description of what occurred on this Jewish festival. Obscure men from very simple backgrounds receive power to preach Christ to their fellow men. The
message is preached in many languages: "And there appeared to
them tongues as of fire, distributed and resting on each one of
them. And they were all filled with the Holy Spirit and began to
speak in other tongues, as the Spirit gave them utterance."[5]

The Holy Spirit is the key to the understanding of the New
Testament Church. The divisions of the Church in our own day,
based so often upon rival institutional patterns of polity, blind us
to the quality of life in the Spirit in that early community. The
Pentecostal sects that have stereotyped and conventionalized what
in the situation of origin was a spontaneous outpouring of power
are no more help to us. The Holy Spirit is "God active in everyday life." Not simply a power nor an attribute of God, the Holy
Spirit is God himself in the fullness of his self-revelation. Father,
Son, Holy Spirit—these are the names of God himself. The Christian doctrine of the Trinity, to be described in the following chapter, is but the human attempt to express verbally the completeness
of the Biblical revelation.

The Holy Spirit is regarded in the Old Testament as the unique
gift given to outstanding men of action, to kings, and to the great
prophets of Israel. Jesus is understood by the writers of the gospels
to be uniquely endowed by the Spirit, as the narrative framework
of the stories of his birth, baptism and temptation indicate. The
dove symbolizes the presence of the Spirit. "The Spirit of God
brooded a second time over the waters, to vivify a new creation
by resting on the new Head of mankind."[6]

It is the Spirit who drives Jesus into the wilderness. His power
in preaching and in curing people is represented as the work of the

---

[5] Acts 2:3–4.
[6] H. B. Swete, *Hasting's Dictionary of the Bible*, Vol. II, p. 406.

Spirit. The discourses in the Gospel of John promise that after Jesus's death and glorification he will send his Spirit to his followers. The writer of the Gospel of John pictures the fulfillment of this promise when the resurrected Christ breathes the Spirit upon the disciples.

What is new in the event of Pentecost, so variously described, is that the Holy Spirit is now given to very ordinary people. What in the Old Testament was regarded as the possession of special persons now becomes "democratized." The prophecy of Joel that in the Messianic Age the Spirit would be given to "all flesh" is regarded as being fulfilled every day in the experience of the Christian community. The special significance of this for our analysis of revelation is that it underscores the community-creating element in the Biblical revelation. What had before in the Old Testament been regarded as a gift to special individuals now becomes a corporate possession of a community of believers, in which all share not so much as distinguished individuals but as everyday folk, bound to each other by a new realization of God's very presence in their midst. Henceforth the prayer of this community will not so much request the Spirit as beg that he not leave them. In the traditional versicles of Morning Prayer the petition: "O God, make clean our hearts within us," is followed by: "And take not thy Holy Spirit from us." What was episodic and temporary in the Old Testament has become permanent in the New Testament Church.

There is a further contrast to be analyzed. The Spirit replaces the Law. The outward yields to the inward. In the Old Testament God is known by the Law, but, in spite of the progressive redefinitions of the Law by legal redactors mirroring new levels of prophetic teaching about God, the inevitable problem of legalism remained unsolved. Much of Jesus's teaching is directed against a scribal attitude toward the Law, with its attendant petty casuistry, and against the Pharisaic blindness of pride and of lovelessness springing from legalism. Higher prophetic insight in the Old Testament had been aware of this problem. Jeremiah, after accepting the Deuteronomic reform of the Law under King Josiah, became increasingly skeptical of this avenue of relationship between God and man. In the later chapters of the book of Jeremiah there is expressed the hope of a New Covenant based upon an inner apprehension of God's demands rather than upon an external code:

"Behold, the days are coming, says the Lord, when I will make a new covenant with the house of Israel and the house of Judah, not like the covenant which I made with their fathers . . . I will put my law within them, and I will write it upon their hearts . . . And no longer shall each man teach his neighbor and each his brother, saying, 'Know the Lord,' for they shall all know me, from the least of them to the greatest. . ."[7]

The community described in Acts believed that this promise had been fulfilled. Henceforth the knowledge of God is not so much to be sought in the verbal transcript of a special code as in a group mind within the Spirit-guided community open to the guiding of the Spirit. St. Paul's well-known chapter in Corinthians has already been cited to show that we know in part. It should also be quoted to show that "if I have prophetic powers, and understand all mysteries and all knowledge . . . but have not love, I am nothing."[8] The Holy Spirit bestows love upon the community of faith. "Behold how these Christians love one another." That love which led Christ to the Cross has been shed abroad in the hearts of his followers by the Holy Spirit. The revelation of love in the Incarnation and the Atonement as the very heart of reality is meant to be reflected in the corporate life of the Church, not so much as an ideal striven for in obedience to its Lord, but as a reality given by the Holy Spirit that seeks expression through the community.

Another way of stating this inner, continuous, and universal work of the Holy Spirit after Pentecost is to realize that the Holy Spirit is not some new reality pointing to himself. He points to Christ.

---

[7] Jeremiah 31:31–34.   [8] 1 Corinthians 13:2.

The function of the Spirit in the Old Testament remained obscure. Now his task is seen to be that of glorifying the Son. The Holy Spirit is God at work in human life, transfiguring the faith of the disciples and deepening their response to the risen and ascended Lord. They become now less dependent upon the days of his flesh. They see that the elements in his life and teaching are meant not as ends in themselves, to be repeated in every culture and situation, but as pointers to the very presence of God, who demands in every new situation responsible decisions and not mechanical imitation. The earthly life of Jesus, through which the revelation appeared, becomes sacramental in the power of the Spirit for ever renewed experiences of the risen and ascended Lord and ever rekindled light upon our personal and social responsibilities.

CHAPTER X

The Church and Its Understanding of Revelation

The point developed in the preceding chapter was that the Church is an organic part of the revelation of God in Christ. Without the apostolic testimony to Jesus as the Christ no meaningful revelation could have occurred. Thus the apostolic witness shares in the particularity of the revelation in such a way that subsequent generations of Christians are dependent upon their testimony to the great revelatory acts of God in history. But the Church so described is the Church of the New Testament. Does the post-apostolic Church have the same relationship to the manifestation of God in Christ? If so, which, if any, of the Churches today is the true successor to the New Testament community of faith? Is there something about the Church that is indispensable for our knowledge of God?

There is a fundamental difference between the apostolic Church of the New Testament period and its successor in any age. The apostles and their immediate followers actually share in the great events of Christ's life and teaching, his death and Resurrection, his Ascension and Pentecost. Their successors can never achieve direct participation in these revelatory acts in history. Therefore there is a normative quality about this primary community of response that cannot in the same degree attach to later and dependent periods of Church history. There is a transition from the Church as an organic part of God's revelation to the Church as a channel or primary instrument for the mediation of this revelation. The writing of the New Testament documents was the means by which later ages could know the situation of the apostolic Church. Thus, by written documents, the Church established a norm for herself in testing the purity of subsequent witness. Too often an unhistorical frame of mind contrasts the New Testament with the Church, forgetting that the Church existed before the written documents of the New Testament, that these writings were produced within the Church itself, and that it was the Church which, by its use, selected the writings that should be regarded as authoritative. Not until about 367 was the canon of the New Testament completed in its present form.

The task played by the Church in the writing of the New Testament and in the formation of an agreed collection of writings can, however, be overstated. This has happened at times in the history of Christianity. It has been argued that if the Church wrote the New Testament it must be superior in point of authority to the documents which it created. Since there may well arise differences in the interpretation of the documents that describe the saving events, must not God have provided an agency to give infallible answers to such questions? This line of argument takes far too uncritical a view of the continuity of the historic Churches with the Church of the New Testament period. Very early the Church expressed its unity horizontally in the living generation by the polity of bishops and vertically with past generations of Christians by the succession of the bishops in consecration and in jurisdiction. Such an institutionalized pattern expressing the unity of the Church has, with many modifications, characterized a majority of Christians throughout the ages and is the type known today by a majority of Christians. It is a most valuable instrument for maintaining continuity, but it is capable of serious perversion if it becomes an end in itself. If so much attention is centered upon it that the function of the Holy Spirit as the bond of union and as the guarantee of truth is forgotten or minimized, then it borders on the semimagical and falls under the condemnation of the God who has rejected many priesthoods and special channels and who "can of these stones raise up sons to Abraham." While succession may be symbolized by a continuity in office the more significant apostolic succession, and the only type that provides justification for an institutionalized succession, is that Christian folk in every age must be true successors to the faith of the apostles. That faith has been crystallized in the documents of the New Testament. The fallacy in setting the Church above the New Testament is that, while it may be said that the Church wrote the books of the New Testament, it did not create the Gospel. That is to say, it was God's acts that called forth the Church and that led the apostles and their immediate followers within that community of response to commit their witness to writing.

The problem of the relation between Church and Bible will never be solved by unnatural emphasis upon either reality as though opposed to the other. One of the most difficult problems in the Ecumenical Movement is the division between the Churches which express continuity in terms of the episcopate in apostolic succession and those Churches which appeal directly to the New Testament as against the historic institution and emphasize almost exclusively the Holy Spirit as the bond of unity. It would appear again that both sides bear witness to important truths, that both are stronger in their affirmations than they are in their negations, and that the Church of the future must somehow comprehend both perspectives within itself. There must, however, be no obscuring of the essential difference between the apostolic Church, which shares and participates in the primary revelatory events of Christ, and the Church in subsequent periods, which is meant to be a signpost, pointing through the early community of faith to the

primary events themselves, and as a channel of revelation, offering
to men, through the Holy Spirit, occasions for direct meeting with
God in Christ.

The Church then has a twofold activity to discharge. Since it is
entrusted with the Gospel it must be sure to bear witness to that
Gospel and not to some other message. The Church must guard
the Gospel committed to it. This task has a conservative and somewhat static side. On the other hand, the Church as a channel of
revelation is charged to spread the Gospel throughout the world
and to make possible ever renewed experiences through which
men meet the living God. This task has a boldly interpretive and
dynamic side. At various periods this twofold function has been
compromised by the neglect of one or the other of the tasks. Both
areas of concern are represented in the New Testament. St. Paul
argues for the purity of the Gospel against any additions to it of
the traditions of men, particularly in his controversy with those
who would retain the Jewish Law as binding upon Gentile con-
verts. In some of the Johannine letters there is expressed an increasing concern for the purity of the faith. That faith begins to be
expounded in doctrinal statements and theological definitions. "By
this you know the Spirit of God: every spirit which confesses that
Jesus Christ has come in the flesh is of God."[1] Apparently there
were those who were denying that Jesus had come in the flesh.
It became a commonplace of the later Gnosticism, a syncretistic
philosophy of religion combining the contemporary world view of
the second and third centuries with occultism and speculation,
that Jesus's humanity was not real. With the Gnostics' inheritance
of the Oriental dualism between flesh and spirit, they doubted that
God would associate himself with evil matter. Perhaps some such
doctrine as this at a germinal stage was troubling the community
addressed by this letter. What is significant here is that the seeds
of dogmatic definition are already being sown within the Church.
Here we see prefigured the long dogmatic battles about the person

[1] 1 John 4:2.

of Christ that both saved the Gospel from dissolution but at the same time were marked with steadily diminishing returns and ended with the Church's attention far too strongly centered upon dogma, which was regarded as the revelation itself.

The second task of the Church is represented in the documents of the New Testament by the boldness with which St. Paul opposes the new movement to Judaism, by the daring interpretation of Christ by the writer of the Gospel of John in terms of the *Logos* philosophy of his day, and by a steady growth of missionary activity. Unfortunately the dynamic and interpretive task would, in the subsequent history of the Church, often be obscured by the conservative attention to dogma. St. Augustine's use of the terms of Neo-platonism and St. Thomas's presentation of the Christian faith in the increasingly accepted Aristotelian philosophy of the twelfth century are illustrations of the creative daring of great theologians. Unfortunately by their time the Christian understanding of revelation had become so identified with the intellectualist type of thought in Graeco-Roman culture that the Biblical understanding of revelation as given in the acts of God had become confused with the dogma originally meant to protect that very revelation.

In its task of guarding the revelation committed to it the early Church forged four institutions. Canon and polity have been discussed. The formation of the creeds and the writings of the Apologists had considerable influence in shaping the Church's attitude toward revelation. The exact origins of the creeds are in dispute, but there is more or less general agreement that they emerged from such simple New Testament confessions that "Jesus is Lord" and from the practice of Baptism in the Triune name of God. The Apostles' Creed, as we have seen, represents the deposit of the apostolic preaching to which a number of clauses have been added. The predominance of verbs of action in the section on Christ faithfully translates the Biblical emphasis upon revelation as the activity of God in history. It is a worthy "miniature

Bible," doing justice to the Gospel by its concentration upon God's mighty acts. When its structure is compared with what is commonly called the Nicene Creed a significant shift in emphasis is found. The old verbs of action are still there, but they are beginning to be surrounded by increasing nouns and substantive phraseology. The language is still Biblical for the most part except for the famous Greek word *homoousion* (of the same substance) that resulted from the Arian Controversy, but the substantive tone or total impact of the Nicene Creed is in contrast with the simpler Apostles' Creed. Behind this development lay the dogmatic controversies of the early Church and the increasing use in theology of the distinctive vocabulary and thought forms of Graeco-Roman culture. This assimilation was pioneered by the Apologists, who presented Christianity as the truest of all philosophies or as a reformulation of the moral law. Justin Martyr continued to wear his philosopher's cloak after his conversion to emphasize this point.

It is impossible to trace here the many currents and crosscurrents in the development whereby Christians began to accept revelation as divinely inspired truths either written in the sacred books or defined in dogma by competent ecclesiastical authority. Origen, who is often called the father of Christian theology, adapted the scientific methodology of his day to the expression of Christian truth. This meant the use of Bible and creed as verbal transcripts of revelation from which, by the process of deduction as from first principles, derivative propositions were set forth. It was significant that Origen chose this methodology from the deductive science of his day, for it set the pattern for theological exposition for a thousand years and strengthened the verbalistic attitude toward revelation. It is interesting to speculate what might have happened had he chosen as his theological method the empirical procedures of Greek medicine then undergoing considerable development.

Our concern with the early controversies is to show their effect upon the understanding of revelation and of the person and work of Christ as these two major areas influenced each other. At times impatience with scholastic elaborations and theological niceties have led men to reject the whole of tradition for a return to the language and theology of the New Testament. The truth in this protest is that the New Testament presents a norm for guiding Christian thought that has been too often obscured in the history of theology, but the attempt to arrest thought at the level achieved in the New Testament is as illusory as bidding the incoming tide to halt. A historical examination of the New Testament reveals that it is not a book of completed doctrine but a collection of occasional writings with many different perspectives on the same subject and, in most cases, a pretheological formulation of the problem. Merely to reproduce the language of the New Testament in subsequent periods is to stultify creative thought both in the sense that Biblical truth needs to be expressed in the ever changing thought forms of the centuries and in the obligation to free what is abiding in the New Testament from its necessary imprisonment in the thought structures of the first century. Theological "archaism," to adapt a phrase of Toynbee's, offers no constructive answer.

In spite of many differences in emphasis and considerable variation in terminology one basic affirmation is common to all the writers of the New Testament: *Jesus is both God and man.* There can be absolutely no dispute that Jesus was a man among men. This is their bedrock certainty. As for the deity of Christ, it can be stated that no writer sees in him anything less than something more than a prophet. Whether he is described as the Messiah, with special emphasis upon his mission to inaugurate the Kingdom of God, or as the Son of Man, with its associations with the transcendent figure in the book of Daniel, or as the creative Word become incarnate, or as the Son of God, or as the great High Priest, entered once and for all into the heavenly sanctuary, it is evident that beyond the dimensions of his manhood there is the presence of deity. Some have urged that the simple confession in the book of Acts that "Jesus is Lord" is all that Christianity ever needed for a creed and that it would have been much healthier had it used only this affirmation. But the Gnostics, who would have dissolved the historical base of Christian faith into a mystical metaphysic, could have accepted such a phrase. The plain fact is that the ascription "Lord" does not tell us enough. To remind us that the Greek word for "Lord" is also used to translate "God" in the Greek Old Testament sets the phrase in its proper context. It would still have been asked: If Jesus is God, are we presented with a case of theophany, so common in Greek mythology, in which a divine being appears temporarily in some creaturely cloak? Perhaps he is divine but not fully God. Or perhaps he "is" God for some limited period of time. Or, approaching the formula from the other direction, it might be used to deny that he was a man, that he had a human life. He might well have been a hero of superhuman stature and as such "Lord" of his cult on a par with other Graeco-Roman mystery religions.

There is no commanding that these questions not be raised in the interests of a simpler precritical formula. The fact remains that these were the questions raised in the early Church, and from one point of view the answers given were simply clarifications of the common New Testament affirmation. The decrees of the Council of Chalcedon A.D. 451 from this perspective were only saying that Jesus is both full God and full man. The problem of the dogmatic decisions of this Council is that this affirmation was enmeshed in the special terminology of ancient psychology and that subsquent centuries would be tempted to give to these official definitions a sanctity given properly only to the One to whom they were meant to point.

The long list of Christological heresies with their definitions has made some people think of the early Church as a vast debating society. Nothing could be further from the truth. What was at stake here was the redemption of man. If Arius, for example, was

right in affirming that while Christ was like God he was the first
of God's creatures then, as Athanasius saw, the Christian belief in
redemption was jeopardized. If Christ was but a creature of God,
although the first and highest, there remained a dark hinterland
of deity behind him and man could not be certain he had been
encountered in Christ by "God of God" and "very God of very
God." If Apollinarius was right that Christ had a human body and
soul, but that the divine *Logos* had simply replaced or substituted
for his human spirit, then redemption was in peril again. Man's
spirit, unassumed by the Saviour, then went unhealed. It is precisely in the human spirit and not in his body that the center of
sin is encountered. If Eutyches was right that there had been two
natures before the Incarnation but only one after it, much as hydro-
gen and oxygen combine to form water with quite different physical properties from those of its constituents, then again man is
dependent for his salvation neither upon God nor upon a real
man but upon some monstrous by-product. If a school of interpretation called Adoptionism was right in its claim that Jesus was
so perfect a man that at some moment in his life God adopted
him, then we are confronted by a purely pagan apotheosis, of a
man *becoming* God. It is surprising how often these heresies have
reappeared in the history of Christianity, showing that they are
no mere arbitrary deviations but (in their way) quite logical oversimplifications of the basic affirmation that Jesus is both God and
man. If the decrees of the Council of Chalcedon are looked upon
in their negative function of ruling out false oversimplifications of
the problems of the Incarnation then they have their honored place
in Christian history. The difficulty arises when the language of the
Council is not regarded simply as a restatement of the basic mystery of the God-man but as an answer or permanent solution to
the vexing questions of the person of Christ.

One of the most troublesome conceptions common to the early
period is that of the "impersonal humanity" of Jesus found, for
example, in the "Tome of Leo," which was declared authoritative

by the Council of Chalcedon in 451. What possibly can this concept mean for modern man whose whole philosophical ethos is oriented against such abstractions as "humanity"? And what can the word "impersonal" mean to him with his rich philosophical background centering about the meaning of "personal," a development in modern philosophy expressed chiefly in the tradition of philosophical idealism and personalism but ultimately inspired by the impact of Christianity upon Western thought? A defender of the Chalcedonian position might argue that the meaning of the phrase was that Jesus Christ is *man* but not *a man*. This only makes the situation more difficult, for the whole modern historical study of the gospels has established, in a way perhaps never so clearly grasped since the time of Jesus's disciples, that we have to do with *a man* in this narrative. The movement in critical study to recapture "the historical Jesus" has had at least the result of pointing to a concrete, historical individual behind the gospel stories.

Although the dogma of the Church has always asserted that Christ is "co-essential with us according to the manhood; like us in all things, save in sin alone," popular presentations of Christianity have often so interpreted the deity of Christ as to overwhelm the structures of his manhood. Any denial of or indifference to his humanity has been, let us hope, expelled forever by the emphasis in modern historical scholarship upon the limitations of his knowledge, the reality of his temptations and struggle with evil, and the human structure of his piety. In this sense it may be argued that we see certain aspects of the Incarnation with greater clarity than our fathers at Chalcedon; at very least we see what the Incarnation must mean in the philosophical language of our day. The importance of the Chalcedonian orthodoxy of the "two natures in one person," conjoined "without change, separation, division, or fusion," is that in its day it carried further the universalization of the categories for understanding the God-man that had in orgin been expressed in the specialized Jewish language of Messiahship. It ruled out false and inadequate ways of stating the relationship in Christ between God and man and left the mystery of his person very much in the same way that the writers of the New Testament in quite different language had done.

The inadequacy of Chalcedon is not merely that it naturally used a vocabulary and idiom that has become foreign to our day but that in its metaphysical interest in "Godhead" and "humanity," conceived very much in terms of Graeco-Roman thought forms, although employed against many of their pagan associations and meanings, it lost an essential element in the Biblical understanding of man and of revelation. Static ontologism, or definitions of being, replaced Biblical dynamism in interpreting man. Conceptual or propositional categories of knowledge replaced the Biblical emphasis upon God not so much as delivering a textbook on doctrine as "meeting" man, challenging him in his moral and volitional depths as well as in his intellect. All of this was accomplished basically through great events in history centering about Christ and mediated to the individual by the historical community of believing response. The New Testament presentation of Christ is at once more pointed in a historical direction, more open to the living God who encounters man, and more aware of the dynamic response of the community of faith than reappears in the translation of Chalcedon. The danger grew apace that correct acceptance of dogma might replace a living response to God revealed in Christ.

The further development of dogma beyond Chalcedon need not long occupy our attention. The failure of the decrees to reunite divided Christendom led to further political attempts to find formulas of reconciliation. The monothelite, or "one-will," controversy with the orthodox decision that Christ must be understood as having two wills, a human one and a divine one, might be described as the logical completion of Chalcedon. It comes, however, perilously close in modern psychological terminology to suggesting a divided personality, a holy schizophrenia, instead of the widely accepted commonplace of our day, "the integrated personality." If we cannot look upon Jesus as expressing in our language the God-intended maturity of human character it is doutbful what we should expect to find in him.

A number of attempts have been made in our generation to restate the doctrine of Christ's person in terms conformable to the characteristic interests of our times. One of these special concerns is our preoccupation with the meaning of history. This is partly to be explained by developments in intellectual history that have resulted in modern man's asking, in a quite new way, the question of the meaning of history. As we have seen in earlier chapters, a revelation that was disclosed in history finally made the culture that grew up in response to this movement aware of the problems of history itself. Here Christology has played its part in the sense that the coming of Christ has broken into the commonly held non-Christian assumption that history is a wheel of unreality or a cycle of meaningless repetitions by giving a lineal direction to the course of history. The phrase "Christ the center of history" is rapidly becoming a theological commonplace of our day. It stands for the recognition that before Christ is the time of preparation in which God is fashioning a people capable of receiving the fullness of his intended self-revelation in Christ. It further points to the coming of Christ and to his atoning death as the disclosure of the essential meaning of life for each man as a person and for the whole system of corporate relationships in which his life is set. Yet its emphasis upon this point is qualified by a recognition that the Second Coming of Christ shows that, while God has disclosed his very being in Christ, there are still great acts to be accomplished before the fullness of redemption will have been achieved. Christ is the light illuminating the darkness of history's strife and evil, but we live by faith that his light will ultimately illuminate areas that for us now remain in the deepest shadow. Christ reveals not merely a new type of chronology superimposed upon our un-

derstanding of clock time but a time which has qualitative meaning. A revelation given in a moment of historical time became
momentous for time itself.

"Then came, at a predetermined moment, a moment in time and
of time,

"A moment not out of time, but in time, in what we call history;
transecting bisecting the world of time, a moment in time but not
like a moment of time,

"A moment in time but time was made through that moment:
for without the meaning there is no time, and that moment of
time gave the meaning."[2]

Contemporary literature, as illustrated here from T. S. Eliot,
makes the meaning of time a central theme. Modern philosophy,
agreed on little else, finds time its most persistent problem. Contemporary theologians like Reinhold Niebuhr and Paul Tillich,
sharing the concern of the age, interpret the meaning of Christ
more in terms of his significance for man as a creature of history
than in the older "two natures in one person" philosophy.
Niebuhr's studies of the dialogues of the self with God and fellow
men underscore the historical orientation of selfhood. Christ is
chiefly described as the Incarnation of God's atoning love. Tillich's systematic theology finds its key principle in "Christ the
center of history."

"It is self-deception, when profane interpretation of history of
the progressive or revolutionary, conservative or organic type con-
siders itself capable of treating history without regarding the
Christological question . . . The old Christological struggle has
been transformed into a struggle about a Christian or a half-pagan
interpretation of history . . . These questions replace the old question as to the relationship of these two natures in Christ."[3]

[2] T. S. Eliot, *The Rock,* from *The Complete Poems and Plays,*
Harcourt, Brace, 1952, p. 107.
[3] P. Tillich, *The Interpretation of History,* Scribner's, 1936, pp. 243
and 261, footnote.

While our concern with Christ's disclosure of the meaning of history is particularly characteristic of our age, in contrast to the interests of the period of Chalcedon, it may yet be argued that we are thereby more in sympathy with the Biblical understanding of revelation than were the fifth-century theologians. What is meant is not that first-century Christians debated the philosophy of history as we do but that God's actual revelation in history is more clearly apprehended by men whose understanding of man gives a dominant place to him as the "historical animal" rather than as the "rational animal" of so much of Greek thought. Our typically modern question is: "What does God reveal in Christ about the meaning of history?" It is probably a safe prediction that future theological writing about Christ in our generation will center even more strongly than hitherto about this concern. Just because we ask the question of Christ's person differently from our fathers we must guard against undue impatience with their questions, for their questions are still basic ones. "What does Christ reveal to us about God?" "What does Christ reveal about us men?" "How can God and man be conjoined in Christ?" These are all fundamental to any definition of history. They deserve to be faced in every generation.

One of the most recent suggestions in this field has come from Donald Baillie in his book *God Was in Christ*. He argues that truths about God can only be described in a paradoxical way. This does not mean that God is a personification of the principle of self-contradiction but that, when men objectify in words the reality of the living God who is known in the "I-Thou" relationship of faith, the derivative abstracts take on a paradoxical character. The Christian doctrine of Creation is an illustration. The belief that God created *out of nothing* is highly paradoxical, to say the least. It is beyond human experience, which never knows absolute origination but only relative or derived origination. So, argues Baillie, there is a "paradox of grace." The better I am as a Christian man the more I am convinced that this achievement has not been my own but the work of God within me. Biography supports him here, for the saints are just those who attribute their saintliness, of which they generally speak very little, to the grace of God. They do not claim a ten- or fifteen-per-cent share in the product for themselves. On the other hand, when we are living at our highest and have attributed the result to God we are never more conscious of our freedom and responsibility. The saints appear as free and responsible agents, not as puppets mechanically expressing movements of divine power. Neither the work and grace of God nor the responsibility and freedom of man cancel each other out, as they are sometimes represented as doing by those whose canons of rational consistency lead them to oversimplify the mystery of life. Both are united in the "paradox of grace."

Donald Baillie means this illustration to suggest how in Christ both God and man are present without conflict, but as expressive of a unified personality. The Gospel records present Jesus as continually refusing to take credit himself for his works of healing but attributing all to the power and glory of God. We have seen that he does not give lectures about the significance of his own person. His Messianic consciousness is not self-reflexive but a pointer to God's plan and grace. When addressed as "Good Teacher" he replies, "Why do you call me good? No one is good but God alone."[4] He makes no independent claims of goodness or power but remains transparent to God. The writer of the Gospel of John repeatedly emphasizes these points in the words he attributes to Jesus. "Do you not believe that I am in the Father and the Father in me? The words that I say to you I do not speak on my own authority; but the Father who dwells in me does his works."[5] In other words, the action of God in the man Jesus is the supreme parallel to the Christian man's free and responsible activity in which he confesses, "I have been crucified with Christ;

4 Mark 10:18.   5 John 14:10.

it is no longer I who live, but Christ who lives in me; and the life I now live in the flesh I live by faith in the Son of God, who loved me and gave himself for me."[6]

"If then Christ can be thus regarded as in some sense the prototype of the Christian life, may we not find a feeble analogue of the incarnate life in the experience of those who are His 'many brethren,' and particularly in the central paradox of their experience: 'Not I, but the grace of God'? If this confession is true of the little broken fragments of good that are in our lives—if these must be described on the one hand as human achievements, and yet on the other hand, and in a deeper and prior sense, as *not* human achievements but things actually wrought by God—is it not the same *type* of paradox, taken at the absolute degree, that covers the whole ground of the life of Christ, of which we say that it was the life of a man and yet also, in a deeper and prior sense, the very life of God incarnate?"[7]

This brief survey of the forms, language, and perspectives of special interest shown by the Church in formulating the doctrine of the Incarnation throughout its history points to the centrality of this concern for Christianity. This development is no excrescence or insignificant addition to the New Testament witness to Jesus Christ as God and man. It is the result of the sincere attempt in every generation to love God with the integrity of the mind. Far from obscuring the "simple gospel of Jesus," theology is necessary to guard its inner meaning, to reveal that the simplicity of God is not to be mistaken for lazy human simpleness of mind, and to help the Church to express in the thought forms of a new day the imperishable treasure committed to it. There is another significance for us in this continued and absorbing concern of the Church with the Incarnation. It is a testimony to the chief locus of revelation, Jesus Christ. Christian men have found that their

[6] Galatians 2:20.
[7] Donald Baillie, *God Was in Christ*, Scribner's, 1948, p. 129.

knowledge of God was being perpetually renewed in Christ as from a never failing spring. When a Christian talks about the knowledge of God he is talking about the Incarnation and Atonement of Jesus Christ.

There is another basic Christian dogma beside the Incarnation that expresses the Christian understanding of revelation. It is the doctrine of the Trinity. At first sight the doctrines of the Incarnation and the Trinity might seem to have little to do with each other. A great amount of theological writing in the past generation seemed to choose the first in preference to the latter. One of the signs of theological revival in our own day is the increasing attention being given to the doctrine of the Trinity. These are not unrelated affirmations: they are organic the one to the other. If the Incarnation may be described as expressing the center of the Christian knowledge of God the doctrine of the Trinity expresses its fullness. It is no mere accident that in the period of the early Church the Trinitarian controversies preceded the Christological disputes. In order to describe Christ as the God-man it was first important to know what was meant by the word "God." Their interrelationship, however, is not as simple as this chronological statement might imply, for men learned more about "God" as they reflected more deeply on the Incarnation. Some very significant elements were added to the understanding of Trinitarianism as the discussion about the person and work of Christ continued.

Probably the doctrine of the Trinity is more misunderstood today than the doctrine of the Incarnation. Attention has been focused on irrelevant issues. The mystery of the Trinity is not a puzzle in mathematics. The question of how one can be three or three one misses the point entirely. It might have been twoness of fourness under other circumstances. The problem is not one of mathematical necessity. It is an expression of the Christian experience of revelation. It is as simple and as profound as that. God was known as the Father to whom the human Jesus prayed as did his fellow Jews. Unless the human piety of Jesus was an elaborate make-believe, and the evidence is overwhelming that it was not, Jesus really addressed God the Father. When men say that God was in Christ they could accept no view which portrayed God the Father as absent from the throne of the universe during his Incarnation in Christ. They were driven to speak of God the Son as having taken human flesh. Further reflection and their Jewish monotheism prevented the easy, but pagan, answer that there were possibly two gods. They knew, as Jews, that "God" is a proper name, not a designation for a class of objects. They had already been familiar with "the Word" and "the Wisdom" of God as his agent in creation. Gradually they realized that any view that God the Father had created the Son in time and that the Son had at some later time become incarnate was impossible. If this easy way out of the problem (and Arius emphasized this point, quoting some New Testament phrases) were true, then they had not really known God in Christ but merely a godling or a demigod. Only a view that emphasized that the Son was pre-existent could do justice, they believed, to God's priority in the Incarnation. And that pre-existence had to mean that the Son was coeternal with the Father as expressed in Origen's teaching of the eternal generation of the Son. There was still God the Holy Spirit, whom they saw operative in the life and works of Jesus and whom they experienced themselves as a reality after Pentecost. Christ had told his disciples that it was expedient that he go away. A previous chapter has developed what lay behind the Ascension and Pentecost. God the Spirit was making his presence felt among men who had never known Jesus in the flesh. He pointed to the Son but not primarily to that historic figure now lost from the Palestine scene. Christ was now universally accessible to all men in all ages. This marvelous availability they understood as the working within them of God the Holy Spirit.

As Jews they had known God by his proper name of "Jahweh." They now knew him as Father, Son, and Holy Spirit. The orthodox formulation of Trinitarianism by the Cappadocian fathers in the

East as "one substance in three persons," despite an idiom foreign to the New Testament, expresses explicitly the Trinitarian experience of the New Testament Church. The specific doctrines of the coeternity and consubstantiality of the persons and the Western emphasis upon the Spirit as proceding from both Father and Son are further attempts to clarify basic questions about revelation. It is significant that where Trinitarianism has been abandoned it has been accompanied in later generations by the disappearance of that distinctive experience of God which is recognizable in the New Testament.

Plainly the doctrine of the Trinity is more than just a theological bulwark. It is the very structure of Christian experience itself. Christian prayer is addressed to the Father through the mediation of the Son in the power and inspiration of the Holy Spirit. St. Paul, in Romans, associates God as Father, Son, and Spirit with the Christian life of prayer and with growth in the new life that makes us sons of God.

"For you did not receive the spirit of slavery to fall back into fear, but you have received the spirit of sonship. When we cry, 'Abba! Father!' it is the Spirit himself bearing witness with our spirit that we are children of God, and if children, then heirs, heirs of God and fellow heirs with Christ, provided we suffer with him in order that we may also be glorified with him."[8]

One of the reasons for the recent lack of interest in the doctrine of the Trinity may well be the problem of language. "Substance" as a word has had such a development in philosophy since the period of the Cappadocian fathers that it seems to most modern people an ill-suited term to describe the essence of Godhead. There are even graver problems about the word "person," which meant in the fourth century something far different from its richly developed modern meaning. It was, of course, just the use of this phrase by the Church that inaugurated a long philosophical development in the word itself. As used by the Latin fathers, its

[8] Romans 8:15–17.

meaning is difficult to pinpoint, but it probably stood for a relation-ship somewhat like its usage today in the phrase "dramatis per-sonae," or characters in a play, or possibly in its legal sense, strong with Tertullian, of a party to a legal contract, as "the person of the second part." From these early associations to its meaning today as a "center of self-consciousness" there is a tremendous de-velopment. The fathers never meant to assert by the word "per-sons" that there were three centers of self-consciousness in the Godhead. This, in their day and in ours, would border on tritheism.

If we are to retain the word "persons" in our phraseology of Trinitarianism, and its deeply rooted place in worship suggests that we probably shall, we must use the term in its ancient sense. The nearest translation of its fourth-century meaning into mod-ern speech would be "God in three modes of existence." This lan-guage has a slightly heretical quality about it, for it was used by Sabellius and his followers to mean that God manifested himself in three successive ways, first as Father, then exclusively as Son, and, third, exclusively as Holy Spirit. This denial of the coeternity of the persons was rightly judged heretical. There was a further weakness in Sabellianism that has not always received attention. He believed that God in his innermost being was unknowable and that the three persons were manifestations adapted to our sit-uation of what might be called the periphery of God. This veiled agnosticism did not do justice to the depth of the Christian con-viction that God had fully revealed his innermost nature in Christ. It imperiled an ethic founded upon love and reduced the con-viction of redemption to a shadow. The one thing that Trinitar-ianism means to assert is that not by human discovery, since man is ill-equipped for this type of voyage, but by grace of God's own self-disclosure we know the triunity of God as being really God and not suggesting some hidden fourth behind the revelation it-self. Any modern use of the phrase "the three modes of existence" would have to exclude Sabellian errors. Theological reconstruction is needed in every age, and our words never share the finality of the revelation to which they are meant to point. Mere repetition of the formula of fourth-century orthodoxy comes perilously close in our day to the heresy of tritheism and language which in that period had a heretical sound more exactly reproduces their meaning for us.

The special significance of the doctrine of the Trinity for our consideration is that it expresses the fullness of the Christian understanding of revelation. It tells us exactly who is meant by "God," not some figment of the imagination, not some neutral base of meaning shared by all, but *the Lord God,* who has revealed not just something about himself that might be of casual interest but has disclosed his innermost reality as Father, Son, and Spirit. This binds the Christian knowledge of God at once to history and to a special community of faith, but at the same time it frees it from historical archaism or ecclesiastical introversion. The Triune God challenges every man not to a long quest for the divine but as the inescapable "Thou," confronting man and challenging him to responsible decision. God may employ many channels of revelation, the Bible, the preached Word, the sacraments, prayer, a simple act of kindness or a compassionate word, a historical event, the majesty of the heavens, or the imperative of the moral law—these and more—but they are *channels* and not *the revelation* itself. They are meant to lead man to "meeting," to confrontation with the living God himself. In expressing the wholeness of revelation it might be useful to speak of God the Father as the *Revealer,* God the Son as the *Revealed,* and God the Holy Spirit as the actuality of *Revelation.* These three are inseparable and interdependent. The whole God is present in each and their unity is the wholeness of revelation.

A rough assimilation of our tentative formula of Biblical revelation, as divinely guided event inseparably united with the believing interpretation of that event, would stress God the Father as the source of the event and God the Spirit as realizing and inspiring the human response to the event. God the Son would be the highest pitch of the formula in which the event is fused into the person of the God-man, the perfect togetherness of divinely guided event and human response. The doctrines of the Incarnation and the Trinity express the center and the fullness of the Christian knowledge of God.

CHAPTER XI

Revelation and Reason

The central core of this book has dealt with the Biblical understanding of revelation. The preceding chapter has been concerned with the apprehension of the person of Christ within the tradition of the Church as the key to the knowledge of God. An obvious criticism of this procedure presents itself. What about the other knowledge of God that man has? What about reason and God? What about the knowledge of God disclosed in the religions of mankind? How about mystical experience as a direct pathway to God? No exposition of revelation and Christology would be adequate which did not indicate at least the lines along which such questions might be answered.

The tradition of scholasticism, both in its Catholic and Protestant versions, has been criticized early in this survey. What was objected to was the assumption that there were essentially two separate spheres, one of reason that could prove the existence of God and the other of revelation that would supply content to the "proved" conception of God. The weakness of the scholastic synthesis is that it divides the spheres of reason and faith unnaturally, tending thereby to misunderstand the function of reason and to

reduce faith from man's full response to "meeting" with God to
the holding of verbally correct doctrines about God. In our own
generation the revival of Biblical theology has helped to make us
aware of the second weakness and to restore the dramatic-personal
dimension to revelation. On the other hand, certain theological
approaches, more concentrated on the continent of Europe than
elsewhere, have denied the right of reason to deal with Biblical
revelation. This excessive reaction is as false to the real togetherness of reason and revelation as the scholastic emphasis was in
separating the spheres. Some current theologies claim to expound
revelation alone, but they are unaware apparently of the use of
reason in stating their oversimplified case or else they assume that
their own theologies are revealed theologies. This latter danger is
a very present problem. If one must speak only of revelation, then
there is almost no possibility of communication with people whose
doubts keep them from accepting Christ. Revelation then would
illuminate only revelation. The responsibility of the Church to
bear a meaningful witness would be considerably reduced, and
the Church, with a recovered consciousness of the dynamic, dramatic quality of God's self-manifestation, would be in the contradictory position of furthering a strategy of static withdrawal
from culture. That such an attitude is a contradiction of the
Biblical drama is testified by such admonitions as, "Always be
prepared to make a defense to any one who calls you to account
for the hope that is in you,"[1] and by the whole method of Jesus
in his parables of using common everyday events in secular life
to throw light upon God's ways with men.

The deliberate exclusion of reason from the consideration of
revelation is a corruption probably more disastrous for Christianity
in the long run than the unnatural separation of spheres in the
tradition of scholasticism. It was at least aware that there was a
problem here. It is outside our scope to develop historically the
steps by which scholastic theologians became convinced that un-

[1] 1 Peter 3:15.

aided human reason could actually demonstrate the existence of God in arguments so compelling as to convince all men of good will capable of following those arguments. It is interesting that St. Thomas, usually regarded as the classic expounder of scholasticism, showed himself enough of an Augustinian in some of his writings to admit that reason must first be inspired by faith before it can proceed to its task of proof. It is doubtful today, in the light of the developments in modern philosophy with its widespread skepticism and disbelief, whether anyone with intellectual integrity can claim an absolute demonstration of the existence of God. The force of St. Thomas's arguments from nature had a power to convince in the ages of faith, almost with the force of "common sense," that they cannot have in an age of disbelief and agnosticism.

In addition to the social milieu that conditioned these arguments, there grew up a false understanding of what reason really is and what its task properly calls it to do. Reason is simply the receptivity of the human mind to experience and the sorting out into patterns of meaning of the manifold of experience. It is wrongly described as a tool for discovery; it cannot discover, it can only deal with what is presented to it in experience. Taking "revelation" in its broadest nonreligious significance, reason is totally dependent upon revelation in the sense that my knowledge of others comes chiefly by their communication with me and my knowledge of the external world is "given" in sense perception. The function of human reason is that it "receives" God's self-manifestation. While it is perfectly true that as sinners we are continually misusing our reasons by rationalization in the interests of the self or by ideological justification of our special group, and that the use of reason, like every other part of us, needs redemption, it is false to maintain, as some theologians seem to, that the structures of reason or its ability to think according to rational canons have been destroyed as the result of the fall. If reason is in as difficult a plight as this even this plight cannot be stated by man in a meaningful way. Or if it could be so stated by a "redeemed" theologian it could carry no meaning to the outsider save by miracle. There is no special language of revelation intelligible only to the initiated and without meaning to the outsider. There is no "holy" grammar that states thought differently for the Christian than for the non-Christian. When it is once understood that "reason" receives its contents from experience, including the reception of revelation, it can no longer be regarded on a par with revelation as a potential rival or alternate source of our knowledge of God. Any idea that there are watertight areas that can be neatly divided between the two is ruled out. Both revelation and reason occur together as opposite sides of the coin, so to speak. The one indicates the activity of God, the other the rational receptivity of man in a unified divine-human act of communication.

The Augustinian tradition in Christianity has repeatedly emphasized the togetherness of revelation and reason. God is known in the depths of self-consciousness. *Credo ut intelligam* (I believe in order that I may know). No type of human knowledge is absolutely without presuppositions. There is no knowledge of God apart from a faith presupposition. It is from this perspective that the traditional proofs for the existence of God must be assessed. They are not, especially in our cultural milieu, demonstrations capable of overwhelming unbelief. They are rather the transposition into a philosophic key of basic Christian experiences. The Christian doctrine of Creation and Providence underlies the cosmological argument that nature must have a first, efficient cause and the teleological argument that the world exhibits patterns of purposiveness. The very experience of revelation itself is behind the ontological argument—an argument from the nature of being that must be examined shortly. In addition to transposing the act of faith into a philosophical vocabulary, the arguments help to establish communication with nonbelievers. They have a missionary meaning. While it is true that no one has probably ever come to a lively faith in the living God of the Bible by a chain of argumentation, no one who has had serious intellectual doubts has ever really had these difficulties cleared up except by some argumentation.

The Thomistic tradition, stemming from the labors of St. Thomas Aquinas in the thirteenth century, has been considerably less clear than the Augustinian on the point of the mutual inter-penetration of reason and revelation. The followers of St. Thomas tended to separate the spheres of faith and reason into two mutually exclusive compartments, related only by temporal sequence. After walking so far by reason one must then have recourse to faith. Many modern Thomists claim utter demonstrative force for their arguments in seeming contradiction to this passage in St. Thomas:

". . . in support of this kind of truth (faith) certain probable arguments must be adduced for the practice and help of the faithful but not for the conviction of the opponents, because the very insufficiency of these arguments would rather confirm them in their error if they thought that we assented to the truth of faith on account of such weak reasoning."[2]

St. Thomas accepted just enough of the Augustinian tradition to know that reason requires illumination by faith in asserting his so-called proofs but not enough of its depth to accept the onto-logical argument as sound. Immanuel Kant correctly saw that whatever validity may attach to the cosmological and teleological arguments they both presuppose the validity of the ontological argument. That St. Thomas rejected the latter and still asserted the former two shows the degree to which his acceptance of Aristotle was not critical enough. The meaning of the Greek use of these two proofs from cause and purpose was derived from the Greek assumption that nature was divine in itself. Everything was filled with gods, even for Aristotle. The Greeks did not believe in a power beyond this world that had, as absolute Creator, pro-

---

[2] St. Thomas, *Summa Contra Gentiles,* I, 9, p. 17, in the English Dominicans' Translation, Oates and Washburne Ltd., 1924.

duced the world out of nothing. But it was precisely this insight of Christian revelation that gave the Christian use of these Greek arguments a quite new orientation together with a new way of looking at nature. That new direction was justified only in so far as the ontological argument had validity. It was the silent presupposition, although rejected, of St. Thomas's use of the old Greek proofs.

The ontological argument is the distinctively Christian contribution to the rational approach to God. It made philosophy conscious of the ontological area of thought in a way that has affected the whole subsequent history of philosophy and was but dimly foreshadowed in some of the Platonic dialogues. The great eleventh-century English Archbishop of Canterbury, St. Anselm, formulated it in its classic form, although it could be said that he brought out explicitly what was already implicit in Augustine.

The argument can be briefly stated, but its proper defense would require a book in itself. Its major premise is a carefully articulated definition of God: "We believe that Thou art something than which a greater cannot be conceived." Its next step is the assertion: "A being who exists in reality is greater than a being who exists in thought alone." Its conclusion follows with deceptive ease: "Therefore God exists." What is happening here is that faith is expressing its movement intellectually. Kant argued that the idea of dollars in his pocket did not mean that dollars existed there, but he missed the point. Anselm's contemporary, Gaunilo, had tried the same tack with an idea about a perfect island, but Anselm replied that, of course, ideas of finite objects in the mind do not guarantee their existence. The precise point is that God is not a finite object among the objects in the mind but just that "being" who transcends the activity of thought. If the doubter says that God does not exist we must point out that, although he employs the word "God," he does not give the word our transcendent definition. Perhaps his "God" does not exist because it is not yet that being "than whom no greater can be thought." Anselm here strikes at the root of most of the criticism directed against God. The atheist, as soon as he asserts that the idea of God is something developed by himself or springing out of this or that oddity in man, is no longer thinking about God but about his own admittedly imaginary conception. Beyond this conception stands a greater reality in thought; namely, the truly existing God. The modern tack of the logical positivists in claiming that "God" is a meaningless word falls under the same judgment. If God is a meaningless concept then their doubt is obviously a meaningless procedure. In order to meet faith where faith really stands they cannot dogmatize in advance about "God" as a meaningless word. This is not a metaphysical sleight of hand but an insight into the nature of the God of faith when he becomes the concern of thought. We can only have had thought about God because God has evoked it. Our thought is not an independent venture that dares to postulate "God." Our thought is responsive to his primary self-revelation in the depths of consciousness. Our knowledge does not create reality; it is here responsive to reality.

Anselm's analysis is really a dialogue between faith and doubt, in which doubt is revealed as utterly dependent upon faith for its definition of God. Otherwise doubt and faith are not talking about the same "God." Both must really agree as to the implications of the phrase "than whom no greater can be thought." This being is not simply a finite being blown up to the nth power by thought. The phrase, so abbreviated as to avoid all incidental accretions, points to the self-transcending movement of thought. Here transcendence does not mean unknowability but the recognition that, while it is really God whom we know and not something less, we do not know all about God because he transcends our knowledge and concepts. If doubt accepts faith's definition, and not to do so means that doubt is not dealing with the God of faith, then it becomes clear to doubt that the denial of God's existence is in the very nature of the case impossible, that doubt is parasitical upon faith, and that the deepest substratum of human consciousness is transparently aware of God. Descartes, often regarded as the father of modern philosophy by his use of the method of provisional doubt, testifies to this situation: "It is not within my power to think of God without existence, though it is within my power to imagine a horse with or without wings."

If the ontological argument possesses the degree of validity which this exposition claims for it, then more light is thrown upon the roots of our knowledge of God. God is not given primarily in our experience of nature, nor is he given primarily in our experience of other selves. Both of these types of knowledge become associated with our primary knowledge, but our primary knowledge springs from a universal and primordial impact of God upon every human being. We believe because he first revealed himself to us. Not an overtone of other types of knowledge, the knowledge of God is the presupposition behind our experience of reality. In moments of deep awareness the self knows itself to stand before God. Such private experience, of course, takes place within a social context, but it is the authenticity of the individual experience that makes the truth of the social revelation convincing and challenging. Such a conclusion will have obvious bearing on the fact that there are many religions in the world and that Christianity has an obligation to offer some account of the fact of universal religious experience.

Another function of reason may be described as clarifying the types of human knowledge which man ordinarily has and relating revelation to this complex. Reason may be used to develop, on the basis of broadly accepted areas of experience, the probability of a revelation being given to man. It may even take us somewhat further in showing that so probable a revelation will have features that separate it from process in general and relate it to history in particular.

The force of the analysis depends upon an ascending order of complexity in our knowledge of our world that is matched by an increasing dependence of the self upon communication being given to it rather than discovered by it. At first glance a stone is a simple object to describe. It can be catalogued as to size, shape, crystalline structure, and hardness. It can be subjected to chemical analysis. It ideally fits the techniques of modern science with its commonly accepted instruments of measuring and recording. (Of course, if one pierces behind the measurements the whole question of the constitution of matter is raised and the intricate problems of nuclear physics become inescapable. The point here being made is that at least in everyday procedure the description of a stone is regarded as a fairly simple task.)

To go one step higher in the scale of complexity, let us describe a tree. All of the previous methods can still be employed to advantage, but the task of description is complicated by the new factor of vegetative life and growth. The tree can be catalogued as to its class, but something quite as unique as "this tree" cannot be so reduced. It still remains "this oak" in "this situation," with special features due to soil, wind, other trees, and sun. In spite of these features the knower can still treat the tree as an object of his experimentation and, as an external observer, give an adequate account of the situation. The poet is, however, by no means excluded from contributing new depths to this knowledge by evoking responses of beauty that would not be strictly subject to scientific analysis. If the stone were Plymouth Rock or the tree Connecticut's Charter Oak, in which the colony's charter was hidden in its struggle against the tyranny of Governor Andros, then new historical dimensions are superimposed.

A dog is more difficult to describe than a tree because it carries its roots about with it. That is to say, it is a creature with a central nervous system. Scientific procedures of analysis are still useful and rewarding, especially physiology. Quite possibly the dog belongs to someone. A deeper knowledge of this pet could only be evoked by its owner because of a relationship of trust and affection between owner and dog.

It is obvious that man is a very complex reality to describe. He can be studied with respect to height, weight, color of hair, eyes, skin, and blood type. His doctor can anesthetize him and, within bounds, if he wants him restored to life, make an analysis of his anatomical organs. The psychologist can analyze his patterns of behavior and a sociologist can study him in his environmental background. All of this constitutes knowledge of the man from an external point of view. But can we really say that we "know" this man? Would not the very heart of knowledge still be lacking? If biography had to confine itself to this material alone how uninteresting it would be. We could only really "know" this man *if he were willing to reveal himself to us*. He would have to "meet" us in conversation that disclosed his inner purposes and values without which the fly-on-the-wall observation would lack the key to meaningfulness. Would we really believe that a surgeon could get more inside the person than his wife or his friends? There would have to be established a relationship of trust and affection before the man would really reveal himself to us. The intensity of that relationship would be in direct proportion to the depth of our knowledge about our friend. The saying, "You can't make a man talk," is profoundly true. Torture may produce some words of information, but totalitarian methods of interrogation usually end up with the victim parroting the ideas and words given to him by his interrogator. Man can be treated as an object but only at the loss of all that makes him really man.

Whatever definition be given to the word "God" it would be a self-contradiction to regard God as less than the highest we know. The highest order of our experience is the realm of persons. God to be God cannot be less than that. He may be and must be more. He cannot be less. If we are dependent upon a man's being willing to reveal himself to us, in order for us really to know him, surely if we are to know God *he must take the initiative in revealing himself to us*. It is the more imperative that he do so since, by the very nature of the case, we cannot find him or describe him by the instruments of scientific test which still had some relevance for studying man.

Thus, if God exists and if he is personal, there is a very high probability that he has and does reveal himself to men. But where? Where do persons reveal themselves most intimately? A man is really known by his friends and by his family. That is to say, persons reveal themselves in communities and associations founded upon love, trust, and sacrifice. If God is personal will he not reveal himself especially where communities of men love and trust him and sacrifice themselves for others in his name? Thus there is a high probability that revelation will be found chiefly in communities of loving response. Where will such communities and families of God be found? Persons are historical beings. Friends do not just develop as trees grow, nor does a man's marriage just happen. Concrete instances of meeting, common activity, a courtship, and a covenant are all historical acts, definite events to which friendship and marriage are responsive developments. In the ordinary run of everyday problems we learn much about our friends and wives, but the deepest revelations come through special occurrences and events, such as the birth of a child or the death of a member of the family. It is then more probable that God will disclose himself not so meaningfully, although he will nonetheless disclose himself, in the uniform procedures of nature and the generalities of history but in special, unique events in history. We can learn much about our friend from his other friends and from books which he may write, accounts of his activity in public life, and letters which he may send us directly. We shall know him still more intimately when he comes to us, as we say, "in person." God reveals himself in the sequences of nature, the commands of the moral law, and the judgments of history, but chiefly he reveals himself "in person." That is to say, we meet him in Christ. By the force of circumstances friends may be separated from each other and prevented from meeting. Their relationship is sustained by grateful memory and the conviction that, if meeting became possible, they could pick up from where they last left off. God, who came in person in Christ, so gave himself within history that his followers gratefully remember him through the Church and Bible. In the power of the Holy Spirit he is no absent friend but ever gives himself to his faithful followers who can experience him as their present living Lord.

The whole Biblical drama which the Christian understands as the revelation of God is not something done in a corner with meaning only for the initiated. To be sure, there is a high degree of particularization in the choice of the Jewish nation as a chosen people from among other nations with their obviously superior claims in culture and civilization, in the calling forth of a faithful remnant within that Jewish nation from other groups marked for their piety, their devotion to the Law, and their zeal for God, and in the winnowing within the remnant until only Jesus stands as the faithful one who is also God in his self-manifestation. The particularizing process, a necessity given the historical nature of man and society, was only in order to universalize that all men might be drawn into a community of renewal transcending barriers of nation, sex, class, and race. There was logic behind this movement, the logic or *logos* of God that became incarnate in Christ. Human reason responsive to divine reason is able to see from the perspective of faith the utter "naturalness" of God's revelation. It was not the revelation that was unnatural or irrational; it was sinful man, slave to his special interests and prejudices, who made the revelation so bloody in the Cross and found the whole story an affront to his reason. There is no enmity between true reason and Christ. How could there be if Christ is the incarnation of divine reason?

"Has not God made foolish the wisdom of the world? For since, in the wisdom of God, the world did not know God through wisdom, it pleased God through the folly of what we preach to save those who believe. For Jews demand signs and Greeks seek wisdom, but we preach Christ crucified, a stumbling-block to Jews and folly to Gentiles, but to those who are called, both Jews and Greeks, Christ the power of God and the wisdom of God."[3]

In this statement of the relation between reason and revelation St. Paul employs what we have called the pattern of continuity and discontinuity. Man seeks to express his religious faith in rational terms only to become aware of the priority of God in the depths of his thought. Chains of subsequent argument may illuminate basic theological problems, provide a language of communication with doubt, eliminate false notions, and establish strong probability both in favor of God's existence and of his special revelation, but they cannot "prove" their case beyond every possibility of dissent. The God of the rational arguments does not point unambiguously to the God of revelation, but from the discontinuity of faith we still perceive that these are not two Gods but one God.

There may be a more homespun way of stating the relationship between the knowledge of God developed by the rational arguments and the fulfillment and judgment upon these by revelation. A doctor, examining a young wife, may predict on the basis of relevant data that she will have a baby. If his diagnosis is supported by the arrival of a son after some months his earlier prediction remains true, although now quite richly transformed by the event. This boy is not merely "a baby," for the event proves richer within the family circle than the evidence of pregnancy available to the doctor.

The main point of this chapter is that reason "receives" the revelation. Indeed, it operates only in a revelational context. The significance of the arguments for or against God is that they transpose faith and doubt into philosophical language. The same is true about the moral argument which has not been analyzed. Even atheism is disclosed as parasitical upon faith.

"Thus it may be permissible to make the paradoxical statement

[3] 1 Corinthians 1:20–24.

that the real proof of God is the agonized attempt to deny God. It has often been remarked that atheism is but a kind of negative theology. The atheist may feel the inadequacy of all human concepts of God compared with that which God would really be, the author of all things, including the atheist. Indeed only one who has experienced God in all his incomprehensible and inescapable greatness will understand the question of the existence of God in its true philosophic import . . . For the existence of God infinitely transcends our thought, our will, and even our belief. And it is precisely in this transcendence that God and His existence can be grasped by us."[4]

[4] Erich Frank, *Philosophical Understanding and Religious Truth,* Oxford, 1945, pp. 43–44.

CHAPTER XII

Jesus Christ and the World's Religions

If the line of thought developed in the preceding chapter is sound, that a personal God will use special historical events to reveal himself, then we should expect this theme to be mirrored in the world's religions. That this is not the case should cause us to re-examine, on the one hand, a line of reasoning that led us to this conclusion and that sprang in the first instance from Christian culture. It should also lead us to re-examine the data of the religions of mankind. Survey in depth of this problem is not possible here, but it may be possible, without undue misrepresentation of the religious alternatives to Christianity, to show that while there are common horizontal structures of prayer, sacrifice, holy men, etc., in all the religions yet there is something empirically unique about the Christian faith. No other religion focuses its claim to revelation in just the way that Christianity does. Empirical uniqueness is not, of course, in itself a proof of truth, but that this special experience of revelation has no serious rival is a fitting confirmation of this faith built upon the special claim of God's once-for-all self-manifestation in Christ.

Modern man, in his search for religious values, is so overjoyed at finding any tradition that stands against materialism and agnosticism that he is quite ready to welcome all religions indiscriminately into his pantheon. Political orators regularly prescribe larger doses of "religion," and some politicians would like to create a "religious" front in opposition to the "Godless" front. This high evaluation of religion as such is partly a naïve failure to analyze the actual situation and partly a quite unhistorical assumption that there is a least common denominator of "religion" in all faiths that is more significant than their differences. Such a perspective is unfair to the facts of the religions of mankind.

It especially distorts the essence of Biblical faith. The prophets of Israel are forever denouncing "religion" in its various varieties as a threat to the purity of faith in the true God. Their phrasing of the commandment, not to have other Gods, springs from a quite different situation than the politician's reformulation of it for our day, that one must have at least one God. Elijah can hardly be pictured as saying: "If you can't believe in the God of Israel, at least accept Baal." Many would say that this is precisely what has been wrong with the Christian tradition. It has presumed to hold a monopoly on true faith; it has encouraged religious intolerance and arrogance; it has promoted cultural aggression against the values of other great religious traditions. Many of these charges unfortunately are all too true, but they have sprung not from a defect in the Christian revelation itself but from sinful, sub-Christian strategies on the part of immature Christians. It is no solution, in the supposed interests of "tolerance," to falsify the empirical data behind the world's religions.

The essence of Christianity is the conviction that the living Lord of history molded and shaped a community in Israel, until in the fullness of time he manifested himself in person, thenceforth to be met through the power of the Holy Spirit in a new community responsive to these divine acts. Do the religions of mankind, with all their deep spirituality as well as their perversions, their noble teaching and their selfish aims, and their universal insights and narrow parochialisms, testify to this Christian conviction? The answer should not be a dogmatic negation in advance, as unfortunately it often has been. The answer should be found in a sympathetic study of the world's faiths and in an analysis to see whether they are pointing to what Christianity regards as central for religious experience.

There can be no question of revelation through history among the religions of primitive folk except in the degree that the tribal life itself is a historical fact. These cultic responses to the environment find their center primarily in the worship of the forces of nature from pre-animistic forms up to the developed national pantheons typical of Greece and Rome. History tends to be swallowed up in nature; it is observable only as the contemporary pressures in the social environment and in the system of inherited taboos. At best revelation here is tribal custom meant only for those within its circle. There is no question here of a revelation possessing a universal claim upon all men. These primitive religions often advance with the civilization of their peoples until they form a tolerant syncretistic system. Such was the religious situation of the Graeco-Roman world at the time of Christ. Such is the situation today of Hinduism in India, a vast jungle of primitive survivals worked over by a consistent philosophy that rejects the historical and swallows up the personal in a vast impersonal pantheism. The tremendous receptivity of popular Hinduism to new gods is seen in the deification of Gandhi in the villages and in the absorption of some Christian values. Rational thought has introduced universal perspectives into a mélange of religious practices. Hinduism, with its lofty philosophy of absolute being, exists side by side with degraded sexual orgies of all kinds. Here is the world's best illustration of "religion" at work. Shintoism in Japan also exhibits, although with less proliferation of rites and deities, the same rationalization of an old national pantheon.

It is important to understand the completely nonhistorical ethos of Hinduism in contrast with the Jewish-Christian selection of history as the primary area of God's self-manifestation. At no place is the contrast more marked than in an area in which a superficial analysis has found verbal similarities. The popular epic of Hinduism, the "Bhagavad-Gita," represents some of the multiple "avatars," or "incarnations," of Vishnu. "Avatar" should be translated "theophany," not "incarnation." Only in Christianity does incarnation mean the unique, unrepeatable, absolutely historical self-communication of God in the form of man. In popular Hinduism there are many "avatars," some in the form of men, some in animals. Of none of these mythical appearances is it asserted that the historical "happenness" is of the essence. Since the Hindu frame of reference exalts the eternal in depreciation of the historical we could not expect anything else. In spite of so-called verbal affinities the conceptions are poles apart. The "enlightened" woman of the West, who argued that if one Incarnation was considered a good thing surely Hinduism must be superior to Christianity because it had many incarnations, failed to see what Incarnation meant in its radical Biblical sense. In so far as revelation means anything more than custom in Hinduism it points to mysticism. The appeal to mystical experience as a form of revelation must be considered later.

There are properly only three living religions that, together with Christianity, possess universal perspectives in varying degrees: Judaism, Buddhism, and Islam. The religion of the modern Parsees near Bombay might be added as a fourth, because it represents in a somewhat parochial mold the universalism of the old Persian religion of Zoroaster, a cousin in time and place to prophetic Judaism. All of these except Buddhism have had historical associations with Christianity, either by way of common backgrounds or by outright rejection and denial of the specific claim of Christianity. It is therefore not surprising to find that all of these except Buddhism find history a primary area of revelation. They will be discussed after Buddhism.

If Christianity can be described historically as a movement of reform that disentangled the universal from the particular in Judaism, Buddhism can be described as performing a similar task of simplification and unification for Hinduism and as making its product available to men of many different national and cultural backgrounds. It is interesting that both Christianity and Buddhism point to great historical founders but, in the former case, in an absolutely determinative way and, in the latter, as a mere accident. The Christian might see some irony in the historical rootage of a great reform movement that was, in the person of the Buddha, quite clear in repudiating history as a primary area. Its later development, however, in its Mahayana, or "Greater Vehicle," form gave a certain importance to history quite at odds with its original metaphysic. Perhaps the crowning irony was that the Buddha who had rejected metaphysics and history and was himself agnostic about the gods became himself the god of the movement. Apparently the historical dimension of human existence is not easily repressed.

In so far as the term "revelation" may be used to describe Buddha's enlightenment under the Bo Tree, it must refer to a basic psychological insight held to be determinative for human happiness. Buddha earlier had sought deliverance from the wheel of fate through the metaphysical subtleties of the Brahman philosophy and by the self-torture of the wandering ascetics. He found it in neither extreme but offered instead a middle way of self-redemption by psychological mysticism. For him suffering was the basic disharmony of existence that cried aloud for consideration. The source of suffering was revealed to him as the thirst for existence, and with the cessation of that desire went the cessation of suffering. By the discipline of the "eightfold path" and the ethical insights of the Benares' Sermon, and by the aid of a monastic community, Buddha believed that man could free himself from the wheel of rebirth and enter the nothingness of nirvana. He himself had turned back from nirvana out of compassion for his fellow men. Buddhist ethics has inculcated a strong element of compassion for all creatures. There can, of course, be nothing here that approaches in depth the revelation of the loving God to his creatures and the death of a Christ to save men unable to achieve their own redemption. Particularly in its Mahayana development in the northern countries of Asia it produced multitudes of savior gods who appear periodically to rescue men, but of none of these theophanies is it maintained that here was an unrepeatable historical incarnation.

Whatever the word "revelation" might mean for the experience of Buddha himself, it came to him as a mystical experience. It was, in fact, identical with mystical experience. In this sense Buddha is typical for a type of religious experience found in all cultures, including the Christian. There are many people today who would reject the Christian claim of historical revelation in order to describe religion fundamentally as mystical experience. Great confusion exists about the proper definition of mysticism, probably because in the West we have experienced a type of historical mysticism mediated by the Christian faith. In other cultures that have not known the impact of a historically oriented faith mysticism assumes a pantheistic form. Sometimes this leads toward world denial, to the conviction that nature and history are illusion. Occasionally an element of world acceptance is retained, as in ancient Stoicism, by equating God and world as synonymous terms. Even in cultures informed by the historical faiths mysticism tends to substitute direct individual experience for the agencies of historical mediation. Sufism in Islam, Chasidic mysticism in Judaism, and much medieval Christian mysticism, as typified by Eckhardt, have recognizably common features with the "purer" forms of classic or oriental mysticism.

The deeper the mystic progresses the less he can describe what he encounters as revelation in the Biblical sense. The emphasis is upon the swallowing up of the finite self in the oceans of divine substance and upon isolation from the concerns of corporate life. What is most characteristic of the Christian belief in God's self-manifestation in history tends to be denied or assigned merely to a preparatory stage for the uninitiated. The distinction between the living God of mercy and a sinful self forever in need of forgiveness is blurred out of focus by their mutual assimilation. The fact of mysticism occurs in all religions, but in Christianity the experience is transformed in a historical interest. Much that is said about the presence of Christ in the heart of the believer uses the universal vocabulary of mysticism, but no person has actually experienced the living Christ by his proper name outside of Christendom. The spirituality of George Fox revealed that he had studied and appropriated his Bible, which had been mediated to him by a historical Church. The Holy Spirit is naturally associated with mystical elements in man's nature, but he points men to Christ. The significance of the theological division between West and East over whether the Spirit proceeds from the Father and the Son, as in the West, or from the Father alone, as in the East, expresses the concern of the West that religious mysticism must be transformed by historical revelation and that the key to that transformation is Christ. At most mysticism can only point toward revelation; it cannot affirm that a decisive revelation has occurred in history.

It remains to examine the "cousins" of Christianity that stress the historical as the primary area of God's self-revelation. Have we here a movement within religion itself which reaches its culmination in Christianity? Just what do these faiths have to say about revelation in history?

The religion of Zoroaster obviously had its relations with Jewish prophetism during the exile and in the period of Persian hegemony in the Near East. It contributed much in its angelology and demonology to the religious background of the New Testament period. The essence of Zoroastrianism may be variously defined as the religious expression of metaphysical dualism or as an expression of the moral law. Ahura Mazda, the god of light, is locked in struggle with Ahriman, the god of evil. Man is challenged to make decisions of eternal consequence before the triumph of the good over the evil at the Last Judgment. Enough has been described to bring out very real affinities with Hebrew prophetism, but the discontinuities are more significant. Zoroastrianism does not know a gracious savior who forgives men who fail to fight heroically for the good principles. The mystery of a generous, forgiving love is not understood here. Here is really a variant on the theme that religion is basically morality suffused with emotion. Revelation can mean here only confrontation with the moral law.

The situation with respect to Judaism is a complicated one, but it is best described from the Christian perspective as a religion that has rejected its inner hope and promise. In its more orthodox forms it has emphasized that God has revealed his Law, an inerrant verbal record of the divine will. The prophets are chiefly valued as the dramatic expounders of that Law. In so far as it has preserved the hope of a future revelation of the Messiah, that expectation is held as a denial of Jesus Christ as God's chosen representative, with the accompanying rejection of the meaning of those Old Testament lines that convinced the early Christian community of Jesus's Messiahship. The existence of Judaism, holding, as it were, the title deeds of promise against itself, is, from the Christian perspective, one of the great enigmas of history. St. Paul wrestled with the problem in a number of chapters in Romans and expressed his understanding of the situation elsewhere as follows: "For to this day, when they read the old covenant, that same veil remains unlifted, because only through Christ is it taken away."[1] There are, of course, modern liberal versions of Judaism which have admitted Jesus to the line of Hebrew prophets but stop short of the Incarnation and Atonement.

Islam constitutes one of the most powerful rivals to Christianity, having claimed for itself vast areas that were historic Christian strongholds in the Near East and in northern Africa. It has largely proved impervious to Christian missions and is struggling today

[1] 2 Corinthians 3:14.

to extend its influence over the primitive peoples of Africa side by side with Christianity. It is best described as a compound of Jewish and Christian elements upon a slightly reformed base of primitive Arabic religion. It was given authoritative form by Mohammed in the *Koran,* which is regarded as the verbally inspired dictation of the will of Allah. It expressly repudiates the Incarnation, although it includes Jesus as a prophetic forerunner of Mohammed. It misunderstands the Trinity in its barren monotheism. Because of its absolute determinism it has, after its period of advance, settled down today in a culturally stagnant situation. The adherent of Islam acknowledges Mohammed, however, simply as the authoritative prophet, never as the Incarnation of the living God.

It is obvious from the evidence that these "cousins" do not make the radical claim to revelation made by Christianity. They are variant forms under religious dress of the deification of the moral law. Culturally "dated" and centered upon Law as the revelation of God, they do not meet him as person when he "comes" into history. The factor of discontinuity is as significant here as that of continuity.

There are, of course, other living religious traditions and great depths of spirituality in those mentioned that have not even been indicated. The description does not do justice to them in their rich manifestations; it is completely just to them in showing that none of them point to God's personal self-disclosure in Christ as the key to reality. With the possible exception of Judaism they do not even diagnose the human situation in the way that Christianity must if it is to remain true to its characteristic experiences.

What is the Christian explanation for this wide diversity of religious experience? How does it stand with reference to Christ? There have been niggard theologies that have asserted that outside Christianity there was nothing save sinful error. Sometimes missions were justified on the humanitarian ground of saving souls from hell-fire. Some missionary programs even today offer only radical displacement of pagan religions, naïvely unconscious of how much of what is imported to fill the vacuum is not the "pure Gospel of Christ" but a culture-bound segment of it in Western civilization.

Surely the answer to the question of what knowledge of God is disclosed within the rich religious life of mankind cannot be a simple: "None." While many religious practices are undoubtedly shrewd attempts to bribe the higher powers there is also testimony to higher things, some insights into the understanding of love and sacrifice, and some genuine awe before the Creator of the universe. The basic problem of the religious life of mankind is the same as the ethical dilemma of every life. Good and bad lie side by side, so confused as to be incapable of clear separation by man himself, but requiring the help of a Saviour God who bestows both the light of revelation to determine clearly what is good and what is evil and the power of redemption to convert the evil into occasions for the realization of good. In other words, the religions need a key to release them from their partial and confused perspectives. Christianity as a religion, that is, considered primarily as a human response, also needs the same key against itself. The real distinction is that the Christian faith is religion in its fullest, most normative form. Elements in the religions of mankind that exist there in isolation, or in neglect, or in solitary domination to the exclusion of other traits find in the Christian Gospel their true fulfillment. That fulfillment subjects the raw materials of religion to the personal experience of the God who was in Christ. Health in the body is the result of the harmonious growth of cells; at times some cells increase at rates that destroy other cells, with consequent ill health. Responding to the magnetic attraction of Christ, to change the illustration, the elements of human religiosity fall into meaningful patterns almost undiscernible before. Christian faith is the fruition of religion. Christianity, which knows the danger of pride, has found it difficult not to become proud in its tensions with other religious systems. It knows that its proper task is that of servanthood in helping members of other religious traditions to see the significance of Christ. It ought not to pretend to know in advance what cultural items must be discarded. It is for the native Christian to begin the painful transformation of his religious inheritance, not for a missionary who is constantly tempted to confuse Western culture with the Gospel. Only in such a way can the fullness of Christ produce in Asia indigenous Christian thought and practices.

Such a resolution of the problem will please neither strict "revelationists" nor those who would dissolve away the historical elements in the world's faiths in the interest of complete religious relativism. Both extremes are false to the Biblical understanding of revelation. St. Paul has the germs for a Christian evaluation of religions when he argues that God has given to all men a revelation of himself in the Creation. This does not mean some divine activity prior to a fall that has obliterated all traces except as that obliteration is specially "revealed" to redeemed theologians. It means an ever-present challenge to all men, no matter what their religio-cultural background. "For what can be known about God is plain to them, because God has shown it to them. Ever since the creation of the world his invisible nature, namely, his eternal power and deity, has been clearly perceived in the things that have been made."[2]

This ever-present revelation in nature and in conscience, as St. Paul also affirms, is always being corrupted because of human sin. Yet man remains accountable and responsible for this sin. Idolatry is itself an indirect testimony to God. If there were no God there would be no idols. Religion is the human response to the revelation of God. "So they are without excuse; for although they knew God they did not honor him as God or give thanks to him, but they became futile in their thinking . . . and exchanged the glory of the immortal God for images resembling mortal man or birds or animals or reptiles."

[2] Romans 1:19ff.

At this point it is well to recall the chapter on revelation in the Old Testament where the point was made that Israel is continuous with the nations and their religions around her but discontinuous with them in respect to her understanding of the covenant. This movement of God into history must, by the necessities of the case, become a special revelation, culminating in his personal visitation in Christ. The purpose of this revelation is that all men may come to know God in Christ. Hence the ineradicable imperative of missions that is placed upon the Church when it is realized that Christianity has no rivals in its knowledge that God has revealed himself in history in person in a great reconciling act of sacrificial love. This task of transcultural witness, however, is not conducted without a confidence that it can be responded to by men who are always, although they may not so describe their experience, being confronted by God in their respective religions. Here in this general revelation in the religious life of mankind is a point of contact for the Gospel and the source of the evangelical call to repentance.

Our "other" knowledge of God really turns out on examination, whether in the arguments for God that have been developed on Christian soil or in the confused witness of the world's religions, not to be so strange or foreign as might first be thought. It is not really "other" but a pointer to the same God. It draws meaning and clarity from God's constant revelation of himself to his creatures but is completed in his self-revelation in Christ. The Christian affirmation that Christ is the source and fullness of our knowledge of God has nothing added to it by negative conclusions about knowledge of him in reason or in the world's religions except a dangerous pharisaism of orthodoxy. Beyond the fortified citadels of some orthodox theologians and some missionaries, God is challenging all men to "meet" him in Christ. He uses even the confused witness of the world's religions.

CHAPTER XIII

Jesus Christ and Our Situation

When St. Paul used the phrase, "Christ the power of God and the wisdom of God," to express the meaning of Christ for all men he directed it primarily to two groups in his first-century world, to Jews who "demand signs" and to Greeks who "seek wisdom." Both in his analysis of the human situation and in his statement of the Christian answer his words transcend his time and have a special relevance for us in the perils of the mid-twentieth century.

The Jews correctly saw the significance of history and the necessity for a special visitation by God in order to cure its confusions and its evils. Their Messianic hope became the form used by God to reveal himself in Christ. However, their formulation of the hope and their eagerness to have a Messiah who would at very least establish their goodness against their evil adversaries blinded their vision and made them unable to receive the true Messiah. The Greeks had not even raised in any profound way the question of the meaningfulness of history because their own interests centered around the rational capacities of mind to solve basic human ills. They sought a wisdom from within the human mind that would either help them to defy the ravages of nature by obedience to higher canons of reason or, in another version, to live in accordance with nature, aware of a fundamental harmony between nature's and man's reason. In either case adjustment to nature dominated their horizon. History in short, was swallowed up in nature.

In a sense the variant expressions of the Jewish and Greek ethos characterize the typical answers of our generation to the perennial problems of human existence. There are modern "Greeks" who are convinced that all man needs to solve his problems is some new psychological technique or psychiatric therapy, some new method of group dynamics, some special educational pedagogy, or some new application of scientific methodology. There are modern "Jews" who would solve the dilemmas of history by the revolution of the proletariat and the hope of a classless society, by the achievement of world government through the spread of democratic process, or by arresting all social change and by returning to some previous expression of particularism such as a somewhat mythical "American way of life." There are probably fewer pure "Greeks" in our world than in the first century simply because we are so conscious of the perils of our history. This intensification of contemporary concern for our historical situation is a compound of many elements—mass communication fostered by technological progress that makes crises in distant areas instantaneous problems of diplomacy, a world armament race between two colossal powers exploiting the fission and fusion of the atom, and the end of white colonialism and the uprising of poverty-stricken peoples. Behind the phenomena that direct our attention to the historical scene lies the significant fact that this development grew in the soil of a culture that was oriented in the direction of historical concern because of the Christian belief that history was the primary area of God's self-revelation.

To such a situation the Christian faith testifies to Christ, "the power and wisdom of God." The linking of power and wisdom is especially significant, for too often these have been treated in isolation. The Christian knowledge of God is the result of God's self-manifestation. It needs to be wisdom in the first instance because man, in the confusion of his sin, sets his goals on things that fall short of God's design. A revelation that self-sacrificing love is the heart of reality illuminates a mind bent on other values and aims. Man is not so far gone in sin but that he preserves some dim recollection that love is the law of life, but if left to himself he serves other ends. There is therefore required a revelation of God's love with power. The fact that God reveals not some verbal treatise on love but shows his love in a historical life of costly servanthood that ends in death at the hands of his enemies is a revelation of power. But this power is not quite what man means by power. The irresistible force of a hydroelectric development is not our analogy. Through the Holy Spirit man sees in Christ a revelation of wisdom and power and then that this wisdom and power is the wisdom and power of *God*. Faith, in other words, is necessary to know God. A man knows God as the Lord of Nature, Reason, and Conscience because he has met him first as the Lord of History. He has met him as Lord of History, not from some supposedly impartial historical perspective, but in the company of the believing community in which God continues to point men to Christ. Most modern substitutes for the Christian understanding of God still show their origins in Christian culture, although the process of secularization may hide from men their apparently unconscious dependence upon this socio-religious inheritance.

Some have assumed that Christ could be retranslated as "our wisdom" without the affront to human pride involved in describing him also as the "power of God." Sensitivity to others' needs, acceptance of others' lovelessness—these are offered as needed and possible goals of human behavior. The difficulty comes in their honest application. I know my duty to be a perfect husband and father and to be a perfect neighbor both to the interesting and attractive and to the uninteresting and repellent people around me. The harder I try the less successful I am. Anxious concern to be the good parent frequently communicates more anxiety to the children than a wholesome relationship should. I cannot win battles over my pride in dealing with my neighbors without somehow increasing my pride in that very process. I may realize the suicidal nature of national and racial pride, but I am so parasitical upon these national and racial structures that I am false again and again to my deepest insights. As a man responsible for my conduct I realize that my successes are only approximations and that these partial successes in one direction often create chains of problems in other areas. I can will the right; I cannot perform it. My basic personal need is release from so intolerable a situation; my basic need as a historical creature is that history shall find a solution for its inner contradictions that both threaten the meaningfulness of history and imperil improvement in the self. In answer to this need the Christian faith presents "Christ crucified." That is to say, because of God's atoning act in Christ, God "accepts" me while still a sinner. He does not demand that I put myself right first. That is not within my power. He accepts me in my failures to obey the ideal, even in my confusion about the ideal itself. The result of such "acceptance," traditionally known as justification by faith, is that with my "self" now centered on Christ I experience new accessions of strength for meeting my responsibilities. This does not lead to irresponsibility but to effective concern. The conviction that such accepting love as shown in the Cross is not merely heroic and tragic, but a revelation of "wisdom and power," strengthens my hope that history will at some point acknowledge its own norm. That norm of love has been disclosed to the eyes of faith in the life and death and Resurrection of Christ. To be allowed to understand God's purpose and design with history gives me courage to face my historic responsibilities as his servant, and yet, because I am relieved of remaking history in my own image, I can face the frustration of my proximate hopes without fanati-

cism or despair. Here alone is that Archimedean point from which
worlds can be levered or, in more scriptural idiom, mountains can
be moved.

There are many ways in which the revelation of Christ is offered
to modern man for his appropriation. This communication of
meaning and power centers around the activity of the Church.
The tragedy is that the pettiness of much Church life, the isola-
tionist tendencies of denominations, the formal lovelessness of its
fellowship—all these hide from modern man the essential reason
for the existence of the Church of Christ. That reason is to lead
new members and old members ever more deeply into a loving
response to God's mighty acts in history and to become thereby
instruments in this generation of his sacrificial, reconciling love.
The Church seeks renewal in the Spirit for this task. It must reveal
itself not as a "religious club" very much on the par with fraternal
and service organizations in a community but as a "congregation
of faithful men." Here the Word is preached. In the services of
worship there are readings from the foundation records of the
Christian movement. A sermon, meant to point beyond itself and
the preacher, invites faith in God's acts interpreted in modern
language in the crises of family and national life. Sacraments are
celebrated in which members are incorporated into this body of
response or in which God gives himself in "Holy Communion" to
the faithful. The historic liturgies of the Christian Churches seek
to bring the worshiper into living recollection and participation
in the great acts of God. The deliverances of the Old Covenant
are rehearsed and the greater glories of the New appropriated,
"having in remembrance his blessed passion and precious death,
his mighty resurrection and glorious ascension, rendering unto
thee most hearty thanks for the innumerable benefits procured
unto us by the same." Our thanksgiving is deepened, our imagina-
tions are quickened, and we offer ourselves to God in Christ for
his service and the service of our fellow men. We receive blessed

and broken bread and outpoured wine as tokens of his body and blood, with the effect that Christ is *really* present.

In prayer our spirits are lifted to the very throne of God, and out of this experience of meeting come new perspectives on life's problems and new graces to meet them. In worship our subconscious regions are exposed to the penetrating influence of religious symbols. Too often the effects of worship are limited, in discussion about it, to the area of conscious, personal response, which is its goal. More attention needs to be directed to the substructures of personality that are being built up by God's gracious influence in order that we may become mature selves. We shall be built up into the fullness of Christ. In all this our knowledge of God is being deepened as our lives are challenged intellectually, emotionally, and volitionally. Our "peace of mind" is not a selfish retreat from responsibility but "a peace that passes all understanding" when responsibilities are faced and life is accepted because God accepts us. The average churchgoer has barely touched the resources which God provides to build up people into the mystical body of Christ. One of the chief aims of worship is so to relate us in imagination to the acts of God that we become again participants in the drama of salvation. We identify ourselves with the earthly life of Christ by assimilating his teaching and life. We see our sin as crucifying him, our cowardice as betraying and denying him, our hope as being revivified in his Resurrection. Like immigrants who must appropriate the events and great personalities of their new country in order to become its citizens, we become aware of our pilgrimage to a new land, we relive the triumphs of the saints, and we repent the sins of our Church fathers. We try to relive redemptively the past in order to meet with insight and courage the redemptive possibilities of our present. We learn to trust God for the future and to work without haste and without rest to help bring that future within the experience of redemption.

Much of the modern Church scene could be described as "God's frozen people." There is, however, evidence that the ice jam is moving. One might add to the empirical uniqueness of Christianity in presenting religion in its most radical personal form, as discussed in the preceding chapter, another distinctive characteristic. Unlike the other great faiths, it has shown a remarkable power in century after century to overcome its weaknesses and distortions and to recover from its corruptions. Here is a testimony to the truth of that unique and final revelation which lies at its heart and is perpetually being purified by the Holy Spirit from the human categories in which it is expressed. Reformation is not in the Christian community a historical episode so much as a continuing process. The Ecumenical Movement is drawing Christian people out of denominational isolation. The Liturgical Movement aims to help us worship more adequately as Christians and to bridge the gap between everyday life and Sunday worship. Laymen's centers are springing up around the world with an emphasis upon the vocation of the Christian lawyer, the Christian statesman, etc., as the cutting edge of the Church in the world. There is a new eagerness to engage in group Bible Study and a growing experience of "meeting" God in Christ in common prayer, group silence, and discussion of Biblical passages. A clericalized or professionalized Church is increasingly seen as a caricature of the Church as the Body of Christ, incorporating within it the whole people of God. Throughout Christendom today there are vital signs of renewal.

One of the more obvious conclusions from this survey of man's knowledge of God is that intellectual problems are not the overwhelming ones. The greater difficulties center around the recalcitrance of the self. It wills to be Lord of all and resents opening the self, and thereby humbling it, to the influences of other selves and to the worship of the Source and Lord of all selfhood. Pascal's observation that the reason for the difficulty of belief is the difficulty of obedience rings true in our lives. God is set upon purposes other than our own. We do not hear him because we will not hear him. Widespread forgetfulness of God in everyday life may be explained along Freudian lines of forgetting what we do not wish to remember.

There is another strategy of the desperate self that seeks intellectual respectability by claiming dissociation from the whole system of Christian belief. The person says he cannot be a Christian because there are many things about which he is uncertain. He doubts that God can be known because the developed doctrine of the Trinity means nothing to him. It is surprising how curious a strategy is accepted by many today who would never think of employing it in other associations. Few people presumably learn to swim by studying the properties of objects suspended in liquids or by amassing a library on the Australian or Japanese crawl. One learns to swim by watching other people who know how and then by trying a few uncertain strokes in shallow water. With increased confidence from partial success one ventures gradually into ever deeper water. One will be practicing swimming for the remainder of his life.

A couple decide to marry not because they have solved all possible tensions in advance but because they are willing to trust their mutual love to lead them through the difficulties of life. A marriage is always a venture of faith and trust, and the deeper rewards of knowing each other that come with time can not be anticipated in advance.

It is so with the life of faith. There is no life that is not being challenged by God, although the person's self-conscious awareness of it may be minimal and may not even yet be expressed in religious terms. God asks only that we act upon the challenge, that we invest our little faith and our undeveloped methods of prayer like the wise servants in the parable of the talents. Our cautious advances will be met by a deepening knowledge of God that arises not so much from thought about him as a possible question mark over human life but as an experienced reality leading into ever more personal "meeting." The sustainer and goal of this pilgrimage is Christ as God's personal confrontation of me and my fellows. While faith is ultimately the gift of the Holy Spirit we are not excused from responsibility for allowing the Spirit to work. Man's knowledge of God is deepened and quickened in his worship of God and his service of his fellow men. There are deep intellectual problems about the Christian faith, but they are only solved or clarified by working them out in the laboratory of the Church and world in the power of faith already held.

It has been the contention of these chapters that man actually can know God and can learn from him God's design for man's disorder. That revelation of meaning and power was given in Jesus Christ in such a manner that it can and must be ever appropriated anew in the Christian community. In Christ we actually "meet" the living God who is Lord of all. One of the reasons why this experience of revelation is not widely realized today is that Christians have absolutized some of the channels through which the experience was mediated to them. This process tended to deflect interest to the channels or means away from the God to whom they were meant to point. The heavy incubus of having to maintain defenses and justifications for the absolutizing of these dogmas, Church institutions, sacred books, and stereotyped forms of accepted religious behavior inevitably obscured the central experience itself and the power of the community to make it available. Decreasing openness to the Holy Spirit meant a law of diminishing returns in the evoking of the experience. Men forgot the treasure in their interest in the earthen vessels which held it. For this reason the scientific development that has emphasized the relativism of the viewer's position offers a needed corrective to Church life. Occasionally one meets a person so dedicated to the Euclidean concepts of space that the newer Einsteinian ideas of curved space are greeted with contempt. He assures us that space is not curved and points to civil engineering and land survey statistics. What he fails to see is that the concept of curved space and a non-Euclidian geometry are apparently more useful for measuring astronomical space. Neither Euclidean nor non-Euclidean categories can be absolutized without distortion. Modern science has become increasingly aware of the highly tentative nature of scientific categories without becoming disillusioned about the realities to which they point.

It is not otherwise with the revelation of God. Our talk about revelation remains subject to psychological, sociological, and philosophical conditioning. But this relativism affects *our* categories and *our* explanations, not the revelation itself. The reason that these channels or concepts existed in the first place is that the self-communication of God called them forth by way of human response. Man studies the Bible in order to meet God. Before modern phonographic transcription reached the efficiency that it has one heard the squeaking of the disc along with "his master's voice." This is an illustration of our situation with respect to the Bible. It is a very human account by men subject to error, to the ethical and religious conditioning of their times, and to the cultural horizons of their period. But it is the only record of the "Master's Voice" that brings us into an eternally contemporary situation with respect to God's acts in history. If we played the old record only to listen to the noise of the disc or belligerently to argue that all the noise was part of "his master's voice" we should have failed to hear the "master." The Bible is meant to be used by the Church to help men meet God. We shall forever in our explanations remain subject to the relativism of our situation, but we know absolutely in faith that we have to do with the true God and that he is behind our knowledge of Christ. We know because he first knew us is the corollary of the Biblical insight that we love because he first loved us.